Vector Search for Practitioners with Elastic

A toolkit for building NLP solutions for search, observability, and security using vector search

Bahaaldine Azarmi

Jeff Vestal

BIRMINGHAM—MUMBAI

Vector Search for Practitioners with Elastic

Group Product Manager: Kaustubh Manglurkar

Publishing Product Manager: Arindam Majumder

Book Project Manager: Hemangi Lotlikar

Senior Editor: Shrishti Pandey

Technical Editor: Devanshi Ayare

Copy Editor: Safis Editing

Language Support Editor: Safis Editing

Proofreader: Safis Editing

Indexer: Rekha Nair

Production Designer: Shankar Kalbhor

DevRel Marketing Coordinator: Nivedita Singh

First published: November 2023

Production reference: 1221123

Published by
Packt Publishing Ltd.
Grosvenor House
11 St Paul's Square
Birmingham
B3 1RB, UK

ISBN 978-1-80512-102-2

www.packtpub.com

To the curious minds who seek to learn and grow alongside us—this book is our shared journey. Written not only to share but also to deepen our understanding, it's a celebration of the power of exploration in the world of Elastic and engineering. We are grateful for the Elastic engineering team, whose remarkable efforts inspire us every step of the way.

– Bahaaldine Azarmi and Jeff Vestal

Foreword

Technology should be about solving real problems, not just keeping up with the latest trends. That's the essence of this book, which focuses on vector search with Elastic. It's about real-world solutions and meaningful progress, aligning perfectly with our mission at Elastic – to create a platform that truly revolutionizes how we interact with data.

Apache Lucene, the heart of Elasticsearch, embodies this mission. It started as a straightforward search engine and has evolved into a crucial tool for addressing complex challenges. This evolution mirrors our commitment to practical, impactful solutions. With the integration of vector search, we're not just adding a feature; we're enhancing how people search and use data, making it more effective and meaningful.

Vector search is vital in delivering exceptional user experiences. It represents a deep understanding of user needs, offering insights that are not just relevant but genuinely useful. Incorporating vector search into Elastic is more than a technical milestone; it's an expansion of what's possible, a move towards more intuitive and responsive search capabilities.

This book delves into the practical applications of vector search in Elastic and embodies a broader philosophy. It underscores the importance of search in the age of Generative AI and Large Language Models. This narrative goes beyond the 'how' to address the 'why' – highlighting our belief in the transformative power of search and our dedication to pushing boundaries to meet and exceed customer expectations.

As you explore these pages, I hope you discover not just valuable information but also inspiration. May this book serve as both a guide and a resource as you navigate today's challenges and unlock the potential of tomorrow's opportunities.

Shay Banon

Founder, Elastic

Contributors

About the authors

Bahaaldine Azarmi, Global VP Customer Engineering at Elastic, guides companies as they leverage data architecture, distributed systems, machine learning, and generative AI. He leads the customer engineering team, focusing on cloud consumption, and is passionate about sharing knowledge to build and inspire a community skilled in AI.

For Aurelia, June, Colin-Harper, and Samendar

Jeff Vestal has a rich background spanning over a decade in financial trading firms and extensive experience with Elasticsearch. He offers a unique blend of operational acumen, engineering skill, and machine learning expertise. As a Principal Customer Enterprise Architect, he excels at crafting innovative solutions, leveraging Elasticsearch's advanced search capabilities, machine learning features, and generative AI integrations, adeptly guiding users to transform complex data challenges into actionable insights.

For Colin, Sloane, and Maureen

About the reviewers

Felipe Besson is an experienced professional deeply devoted to domains of relevance and Machine Learning Engineering. He holds a Master's degree in Computer Science from the University of Sao Paulo and has a decade of experience in E-commerce Search. As a Relevance Engineer, Felipe focuses on having a good balance of data science and engineering skills to become better in his role and push the boundaries of information retrieval. He also had the opportunity to share some of his experience at great data conferences like Berlin Buzzwords, MICES, and Haystack, contributing to the practical side of search components. Currently, Felipe drives the Relevance Engineering discipline at Shopify's Discovery experiences team.

Jenny Morris is a software technologist with over 20 years of experience. She is dedicated to developing effective go-to-market strategies that enable customers to leverage technology for their business goals. She loves working closely with customers, understanding their needs, and crafting solutions to help them succeed. With a strong background in application development, Jenny still finds coding to be a source of genuine creative satisfaction.

Table of Contents

Part 1: Fundamentals of Vector Search

1

2

Part 2: Advanced Applications and Performance Optimization

3

4

Part 3: Specialized Use Cases

5

6

7

Next Generation of Observability Powered by Vectors   123

8

The Power of Vectors and Embedding in Bolstering Cybersecurity   141

Part 4: Innovative Integrations and Future Directions

9

10

Preface

Hello, and welcome to the dynamic world of Vector Search with Elastic—a realm where the precision and power of vector-based search technologies redefine the boundaries of data analysis and retrieval. In this rapidly evolving landscape, Elastic is a pivotal platform, transforming the way we interact with and understand large datasets across various domains. In this book, we will explore vectors and embeddings that are central to modern machine learning and are revolutionizing search functionalities within Elasticsearch. From the basic introduction of vector concepts to their advanced applications in cybersecurity and conversational AI, each chapter is a step deeper into this intriguing world.

The journey through this book is not just about understanding the technicalities; it's about appreciating the broader impact of these technologies. We cover how vectors enhance image search, bringing a new level of precision and relevance. We look into the critical role of vectors in safeguarding sensitive data and explore their growing significance in the context of observability, where they simplify and enhance system monitoring. A key aspect of this journey is the practical application of these concepts. The book not only addresses the theoretical underpinnings but also provides hands-on insights into implementing these solutions. Whether it's tuning the performance of Elasticsearch, managing complex models, or integrating advanced features like Retrieval Augmented Generation, the chapters offer a comprehensive guide to leverage the full potential of Elastic Vector Search.

Drawing from a rich well of experience and real-world applications, this book is not just a technical guide but a window into the future of data search and analysis. As the landscape of data and technology continues to evolve, the insights and knowledge shared here will be invaluable for anyone looking to stay ahead in the field of search and data analysis.

As you read this book, you'll learn about Elastic's features and see how vector search is changing the way we handle data. This book is written for data professionals like you, providing clear, useful information to improve your skills in this exciting area.

Who this book is for

This book is ideal for several groups interested in learning about Vector Search with Elastic:

- Data scientists and analysts: Those who want to deepen their understanding of vector search technologies and apply these concepts to complex data sets will find this book immensely useful. It provides practical insights into leveraging vectors for more nuanced data analysis and search functionalities.

- Elasticsearch developers: Professionals already working with Elasticsearch will discover advanced techniques to augment their current skills. This book covers everything from foundational concepts to more advanced applications like cybersecurity and chatbot enhancement, offering a comprehensive learning path.

- IT and data management professionals: For those tasked with managing and safeguarding data, this book offers essential knowledge on using vector search for purposes like redacting sensitive information and optimizing data search systems.

- Tech enthusiasts and students: Anyone with a keen interest in the latest in search technology and its applications across various fields will find this book a valuable resource. It provides a clear, accessible introduction to the world of vector search, along with practical applications.

By reading this book, you'll gain not only theoretical knowledge but also practical skills to implement and innovate with vector search in Elastic, enhancing both your personal and professional data management capabilities.

What this book covers

Chapter 1, Introduction to Vectors and Embeddings, covers the essentials of embeddings in machine learning.

Chapter 2, Getting Started with Vector Search in Elastic, explores the evolution of search in Elastic, from traditional keyword-based methods to advanced vector search.

Chapter 3, Model Management and Vector Considerations in Elastic, dives into managing embedding models in Elasticsearch, exploring Hugging Face's platform, Elastic's Eland library, and integration strategies.

Chapter 4, Performance Tuning—Working with Data, delves into optimizing vector search performance in Elasticsearch using ML model deployment tuning and node capacity estimation. This chapter will also cover load testing with Rally and troubleshooting kNN search response times.

Chapter 5, Image Search, explores the advancing field of image similarity search and its growing significance in discovery applications.

Chapter 6, Redacting Personal Identifiable Information Using Elasticsearch, covers how to build and tailor a PII Redaction Pipeline in Elasticsearch, crucial for data privacy and security.

Chapter 7, Next Generation of Observability Powered by Vectors, delves into integrating vectors with observability on the Elastic platform, focusing on log analytics, metric analytics, and application performance monitoring.

Chapter 8, The Power of Vectors and Embedding in Bolstering Cybersecurity, explores Elastic Learned Sparse EncodeR (ELSER) and its role in semantic search for cybersecurity. It explains ELSER's capabilities in text analysis and phishing detection.

Chapter 9, Retrieval Augmented Generation with Elastic, dives into Retrieval Augmented Generation (RAG) in Elastic, blending lexical, vector, and contextual searches.

Chapter 10, Building an Elastic Plugin for ChatGPT, shows how to enhance ChatGPT's context awareness with Elasticsearch and Embedchain, creating a Dynamic Contextual Layer (DCL) for up-to-date information retrieval.

To get the most out of this book

To fully benefit from this book, readers should possess a basic understanding of Elasticsearch operations, fundamental Python programming skills, and a general familiarity with search concepts. This foundational knowledge will enable readers to more effectively grasp the advanced techniques and applications discussed throughout the book.

Software/hardware covered in the book	Operating system requirements
Elasticsearch 8.11+	Windows, macOS, or Linux
Python 3.9+	
Jupyter Notebook	

If you are using the digital version of this book, we advise you to type the code yourself or access the code from the book's GitHub repository (a link is available in the next section). Doing so will help you avoid any potential errors related to the copying and pasting of code.

Download the example code files

You can download the example code files for this book from GitHub at `https://github.com/PacktPublishing/Vector-Search-for-Practitioners-with-Elastic`. If there's an update to the code, it will be updated in the GitHub repository.

We also have other code bundles from our rich catalog of books and videos available at `https://github.com/PacktPublishing/`. Check them out!

Conventions used

There are a number of text conventions used throughout this book.

`Code in text`: Indicates code words in text, database table names, folder names, filenames, file extensions, pathnames, dummy URLs, user input, and Twitter handles. Here is an example: " The default pipeline uses the `dslim/bert-base-NER` model from Hugging Face."

A block of code is set as follows:

```
{'_source':
 {
'redacted': '<PER> called in from 001-<PHONE>x1311. Their account
number is <SSN>'
'status': 'active'
}
```

Bold: Indicates a new term, an important word, or words that you see onscreen. For instance, words in menus or dialog boxes appear in **bold**. Here is an example: "The library is built on top of the official Elasticsearch Python client and extends the **pandas API** to Elasticsearch."

> **Tips or important notes**
> Appear like this.

Get in touch

Feedback from our readers is always welcome.

General feedback: If you have questions about any aspect of this book, email us at customercare@packtpub.com and mention the book title in the subject of your message.

Errata: Although we have taken every care to ensure the accuracy of our content, mistakes do happen. If you have found a mistake in this book, we would be grateful if you would report this to us. Please visit www.packtpub.com/support/errata and fill in the form.

Piracy: If you come across any illegal copies of our works in any form on the internet, we would be grateful if you would provide us with the location address or website name. Please contact us at copyright@packt.com with a link to the material.

If you are interested in becoming an author: If there is a topic that you have expertise in and you are interested in either writing or contributing to a book, please visit authors.packtpub.com.

Share Your Thoughts

Once you've read *Vector Search for Practitioners with Elastic*, we'd love to hear your thoughts! Scan the QR code below to go straight to the Amazon review page for this book and share your feedback.

https://packt.link/r/1805121022

Your review is important to us and the tech community and will help us make sure we're delivering excellent quality content.

Download a free PDF copy of this book

Thanks for purchasing this book!

Do you like to read on the go but are unable to carry your print books everywhere?

Is your eBook purchase not compatible with the device of your choice?

Don't worry, now with every Packt book you get a DRM-free PDF version of that book at no cost.

Read anywhere, any place, on any device. Search, copy, and paste code from your favorite technical books directly into your application.

The perks don't stop there, you can get exclusive access to discounts, newsletters, and great free content in your inbox daily

Follow these simple steps to get the benefits:

1. Scan the QR code or visit the link below

https://packt.link/free-ebook/9781805121022

2. Submit your proof of purchase
3. That's it! We'll send your free PDF and other benefits to your email directly

Part 1: Fundamentals of Vector Search

Explore the foundational elements of vector search with Elastic in this section. Beginning with an introduction to vectors and embeddings, this part lays the groundwork to understand their role in data representation and search. This part is essential for grasping the basic concepts and methodologies that form the bedrock of advanced vector search techniques, tailored for newcomers and experienced practitioners alike.

This part has the following chapters:

- *Chapter 1, Introduction to Vectors and Embeddings*
- *Chapter 2, Getting Started with Vector Search in Elastic*

1

Introduction to Vectors and Embeddings

In this first chapter, we will dive into the fascinating world of embeddings, or vectors, and their diverse applications across various domains. We'll introduce the concept of embeddings, which help represent complex data and enable powerful **machine learning** (**ML**) models to analyze and process that data. You'll learn about the roles of supervised and unsupervised learning in creating embeddings and the challenges addressed by vectors. Moreover, we'll discuss examples illustrating the broad applications of vector representation in different fields. We'll also introduce you to the ecosystem of tools and platforms that enhance the developer experience when working with vector search, including Hugging Face and various backend considerations.

As we delve deeper into this chapter, you'll discover the rapidly evolving market landscape and platforms that facilitate the implementation of vector search. We'll explore a range of use cases and application domains, such as named entity recognition, sentiment analysis, text classification, question answering, and text summarization. Lastly, we'll examine the role that Elastic is playing in this space by integrating vectors into the Elasticsearch realm, with applications in search and cybersecurity. Throughout this chapter, you'll gain a solid understanding of the foundations of vector representation and its applications, setting the stage for a more in-depth exploration of the practical aspects of implementing vector search with Elasticsearch in the following chapters.

Accordingly, we will cover the following topics in this chapter:

- Supervised versus unsupervised learning
- Use cases and domains of application
- How is Elastic playing a role in this space?
- How is this book going to help you?

Exploring the roles of supervised and unsupervised learning in vector search

Supervised learning is a method in ML where a model learns from labeled data to determine a mapping between input features and output labels. During the training process, the model adjusts its parameters to minimize the error between its predictions and the true labels. Supervised learning is widely used in various applications, such as image classification, speech recognition, and **natural language processing** (**NLP**). One of the key challenges with supervised learning is that a curated labeled dataset must be provided to train the model.

Unsupervised learning, on the other hand, involves discovering patterns and structures in input data without using labeled examples. This type of learning focuses on finding similarities, differences, or underlying structures within the data by using techniques such as clustering, dimensionality reduction, and density estimation. Unsupervised learning is commonly applied in tasks such as anomaly detection, data compression, and feature extraction.

In the context of vector search and NLP, supervised learning can be used to generate word or sentence embeddings by training a model to predict the context of a given word based on its neighboring words or to classify documents into predefined categories. This approach can help capture semantic and syntactic relationships in the text, making the resulting embeddings useful for various NLP tasks. Unsupervised learning, on the other hand, can be employed to generate embeddings by identifying patterns and similarities in textual data, such as word co-occurrence information. Models such as word2vec and GloVe leverage unsupervised learning to create dense vector representations that can be used for vector search and other NLP applications.

What's an embedding/vector?

Embeddings or vectors play a crucial role in vector search and NLP tasks by transforming complex data into numerical representations. These mathematical representations of words, phrases, documents, images, video, or sound in a continuous vector space capture the semantic and syntactic relationships between elements, enabling effective processing and analysis by ML algorithms. Applications of these vector representations include sentiment analysis, machine translation, text classification, image recognition, object detection, and image retrieval. The following diagram represents the overall process of taking data, applying the ML process, and domain of applications:

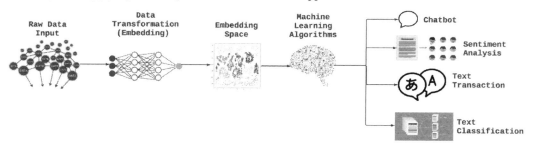

Figure 1.1: Machine learning pipeline

In NLP, word, sentence, and document embeddings serve as vector representations of textual information, allowing algorithms to process and understand text more effectively. Similarly, computer vision applications represent images as high-dimensional vectors, with each pixel value corresponding to a specific dimension. Other domains, such as social networks, biological systems, and recommendation systems, also benefit from vector representations. For example, social network users and their connections can be encoded as graph embeddings that capture the structure and dynamics of the network. With recommendation systems, both users and items can be represented as vectors, allowing for the computation of similarities and preferences.

The ability to represent the world with vectors enables the development of powerful ML models and applications that can provide valuable insights and predictions across various domains.

What challenges are vectors solving?

BM25 is a widely used text retrieval algorithm based on probabilistic information retrieval theory. It ranks documents based on the frequency of query terms in the document, taking into account factors such as term frequency, inverse document frequency, and document length normalization. While BM25 has been effective in traditional search applications, it has some limitations. For example, BM25 relies heavily on exact term matches, which can lead to less relevant results when dealing with synonyms, misspellings, or subtle semantic variations. Additionally, BM25 does not capture the contextual relationships between words, making it less effective at understanding the meaning of phrases or sentences.

Vector search, which includes both exact match and **approximate nearest neighbor (ANN)** search, addresses some of the limitations of BM25 by leveraging high-dimensional vectors generated from modern embedding models. These vectors capture the semantic and contextual relationships between words, phrases, or even whole documents. In vector search, the similarity between query and document vectors is used to determine relevance, going beyond exact term matching. As a result, vector search can return more relevant results for queries with synonyms, misspellings, or different phrasings. Exact match vector search ensures the most similar vectors are returned, while ANN search offers a more scalable approach with a trade-off between accuracy and speed. By focusing on the underlying meaning and context, vector search offers a more nuanced approach to information retrieval that can better understand and respond to the complexities of natural language.

Here are some examples of applications of vector search:

- **E-commerce product search**: Customers find relevant products even if they use different terminology or misspellings in their search queries, providing a more effective shopping experience.

- **Document retrieval**: Users can find documents with similar content, context, or topics, even when the exact words used in the query do not appear in the document, enhancing the effectiveness of search engines and knowledge management systems.

- **Question-answering systems**: Vector search can match user queries to potential answers in large datasets, enabling more accurate and contextually relevant responses in chatbots or AI-based customer support systems.

- **Image recognition and retrieval**: Images can be represented as high-dimensional vectors to simplify image recognition and retrieval. Vector search can find visually similar images in large datasets, enabling applications such as reverse image search, duplicate detection, and visual recommendation systems.

- **Music recommendation**: With audio represented as vectors, vector search can identify tracks with similar features or styles, helping users discover new music based on their preferences and listening habits.

- **Security and User and Entity Behavior Analytics (UEBA)**: In the field of security and SecOps, vector search can be utilized for UEBA to identify patterns and relationships in large datasets containing network traffic, logs, user activities, and other security-related data. By representing users as vectors and leveraging vector search, analysts can efficiently uncover hidden connections and detect potential threats, anomalies, or malicious activities that may not be easily discernible through traditional search methods, thus improving the overall security posture of an organization.

Given the various ways to start developing a vector search project, we will now see the main components we need to know about and what the developer experience looks like.

The developer experience

Selecting the appropriate vector model for the developer's use case is a crucial initial step for developers working on a vector search project. The choice of model, such as a pre-trained BERT model or a custom-trained model, depends on the specific requirements and constraints of the project. Developers need to consider factors such as the size and nature of the dataset, the expected search performance, and the resources available for training and fine-tuning the model. A thorough evaluation of different models should be carried out to ensure the chosen model provides relevant results when used with the **k-nearest neighbors** (**kNN**) search. In kNN, the "k" refers to the number of nearest neighbors in the feature space that the algorithm considers when making predictions – providing a user-defined parameter to adjust the granularity of the search or classification process.

Once the appropriate vector model has been selected, developers need to load the model into a vector database such as Elasticsearch. This involves configuring the database to work with the chosen model and specifying the necessary settings and parameters to enable the model to be stored and deployed. The following diagram shows the workflow, where the model is pulled from a model registry (Hugging Face) and loaded into the vector database:

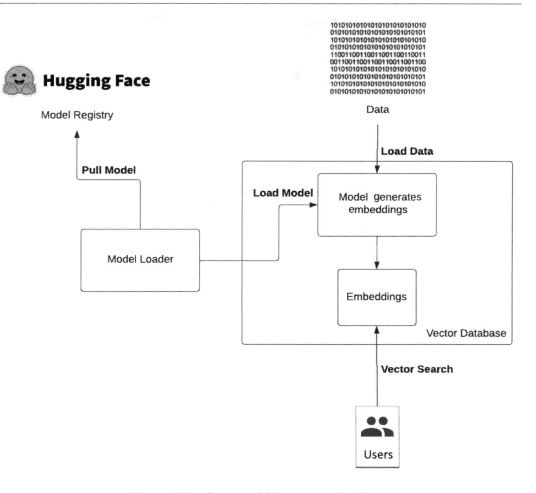

Figure 1.2: Loading a model into a vector database

This diagram also shows that the data that's coming in is going through the loaded model to generate the embeddings on which users are running vector search queries.

Preparing the database to store vectors involves creating an index with the appropriate mappings and settings that define how the vectors will be stored and queried. In the case of Elasticsearch, this involves configuring a field with the `dense_vector` type. Developers need to specify the vector dimensions, similarity measures, and other parameters relevant to their use case, ensuring that the database can efficiently handle vector search operations.

Once the database has been set up, as can be seen in the previous diagram, developers can generate vectors for the dataset by applying the model to new data as it is ingested or to existing data. The process involves passing the textual data through the model to obtain dense vector representations that capture the semantic and syntactic relationships between words and phrases.

Developers also need to prepare a system or process for generating vectors for new queries. This typically involves creating an API or service that takes a user query as input, processes it using the same vector model, and generates a corresponding vector representation. This vector can then be used to perform a kNN or exact match search on the database to retrieve the most relevant results. In Elasticsearch, users can send strings to the `_infer` endpoint, specifying an appropriate model, and get a vector back as part of the response.

With the model deployed and vectors created, load testing the environment is essential to ensure that the vector search system can handle the expected query load. There are specific vector search system resources, such as RAM and CPU threads, that must be considered. Developers should simulate realistic user traffic and query patterns to evaluate the system's performance under various conditions. This helps identify potential bottlenecks and areas for optimization, ensuring that the system remains performant and responsive.

Testing the relevance of search results is crucial for ensuring that the vector search system meets the needs of end users. Developers should work closely with domain experts or users to evaluate the quality of search results and fine-tune the model or search parameters as needed. This iterative process helps improve the overall effectiveness of the vector search system.

Once the vector search system is in production, ongoing monitoring is necessary to ensure optimal query performance. Developers and operators should regularly monitor the system for performance issues, resource usage, and potential errors. They may also need to adjust search parameters, update models, or retrain the system based on user feedback and changing requirements. This ongoing process helps keep the vector search system up to date and relevant for end users.

Hugging Face

Hugging Face is a leading AI research organization that has played a pivotal role in the development and widespread adoption of modern embedding and NLP models. Through their groundbreaking work in NLP, Hugging Face has made significant contributions to the field by democratizing access to state-of-the-art models, resources, and tools for developers, researchers, and businesses alike. Here is a sneak peek of the Hugging Face community landing page:

 **Hugging Face**   Q Search models, datasets, users...

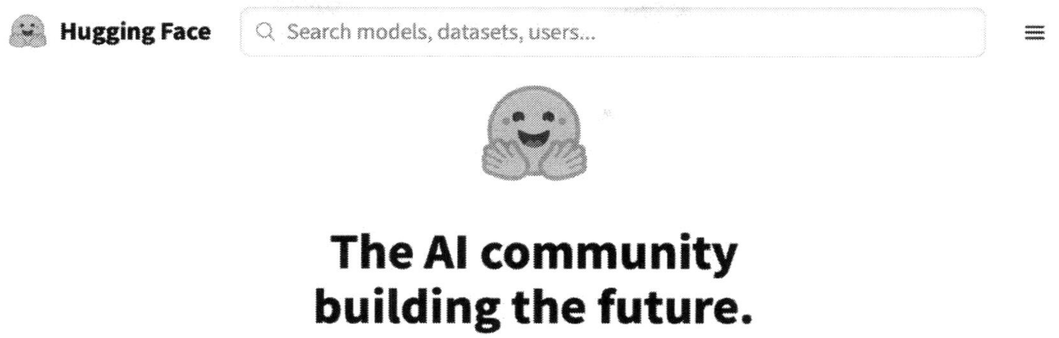

The AI community building the future.

Figure 1.3: Hugging Face community landing page

One of the key offerings by Hugging Face is the Model Hub, a centralized repository of pre-trained models for various NLP tasks. The Model Hub enables developers to easily discover, download, and fine-tune models for their specific use cases. By providing a wide range of models, from BERT and GPT to T5 and RoBERTa, Hugging Face has made it easier for developers to experiment with and integrate advanced NLP capabilities into their applications, including vector search. The Model Hub also offers a platform for researchers and developers to share their custom models, fostering collaboration and knowledge exchange within the community.

Hugging Face has played an instrumental role in the development of the Transformers library, a popular open source Python library for training and using transformer-based models. The Transformers library provides an easy-to-use API for working with state-of-the-art NLP models, abstracting away the complexity and allowing developers to focus on their specific tasks. By offering an extensive collection of pre-built models, tokenizers, and utilities, the Transformers library has significantly accelerated the development and adoption of modern NLP techniques in various applications.

The Hugging Face Datasets library is another valuable resource provided by the organization. This library offers a collection of over a thousand datasets for NLP and ML tasks, making it easier for developers and researchers to access and work with high-quality data. The Datasets library provides tools for data preprocessing, manipulation, and evaluation, simplifying the process of preparing data for model training and fine-tuning.

Hugging Face has developed a comprehensive, free training course that covers the fundamentals of NLP, utilizing the libraries and resources available within the Hugging Face ecosystem. The course includes examples of using community-provided models, as well as guidance on fine-tuning those models for specific tasks and datasets, making it an invaluable resource for developers and enthusiasts alike.

The market landscape and how it has accelerated the developer experience

In recent years, there has been a surge in platforms offering partially and fully managed databases designed specifically for vector search use cases. This proliferation of options makes it an exciting time for developers to explore, experiment with, and implement vector search projects at both individual and organizational levels. The following selection of platforms showcases the ease with which vector search can be implemented today. It is important to note that the companies listed here are not the only players in the market, nor are they the sole means of implementing vector search. They are presented simply to provide you with a glimpse of the current marketplace.

Pinecone

Pinecone is a managed vector database service specifically designed for large-scale vector search and similarity applications. As a managed service, it excels in simplifying deployment and maintenance, allowing developers to focus on their applications without worrying about infrastructure management. Pinecone supports a wide range of distance metrics, such as cosine similarity and Euclidean distance, and offers built-in support for deduplication and filtering. However, as a managed service, Pinecone might not be as customizable as self-hosted solutions, and its pricing structure could be a limitation for some users, particularly those with tight budget constraints or unpredictable workloads.

Vespa.ai

Vespa.ai is an open source, scalable, and real-time search engine that supports vector search, as well as text search and structured data search. Vespa is versatile as it can handle a variety of use cases ranging from recommendation systems to news article search. It offers an expressive query language, supports custom ranking functions, and allows for real-time indexing. However, Vespa's versatility may also be a weakness for some users, as its complexity can make it more challenging to set up and configure compared to databases specifically designed for vector search.

Milvus

Milvus is an open source vector similarity search engine that is built on top of other popular open source technologies such as FAISS and NMSLIB. Milvus is designed for high performance and scalability, providing support for various similarity search algorithms and distance metrics. It is capable of handling billions of vectors and can be easily integrated with ML frameworks such as TensorFlow and PyTorch. However, some users may find Milvus to have a steeper learning curve, particularly if they are not already familiar with the underlying technologies. Additionally, Milvus is focused primarily on vector search and does not support other search modalities, which may limit its applicability for certain use cases that require a combination of vector, text, and structured data search.

Weaviate

Weaviate is an open source, GraphQL-based vector search engine that enables users to search for data using natural language queries. One of Weaviate's strengths is its focus on semantic search, making it well-suited for applications where understanding the meaning of a query is important. It also supports schema-based data modeling, allowing users to define the structure of their data and the relationships between different entities. However, Weaviate's focus on semantic search (vector or hybrid search) and its reliance on GraphQL may introduce complexity for some users, particularly those who are not familiar with these concepts.

Elasticsearch

Elasticsearch v8+ from Elastic.co supports dense vector storage for ANN and exact match search, providing a scalable approach to vector search on large datasets. Unlike exact match nearest neighbor search, ANN trades perfect accuracy for speed, making it more efficient with high-dimensional vectors. Elasticsearch employs the **Hierarchical Navigable Small World** (**HNSW**) graphs ANN algorithm, boasting strong performance and widespread industry use. Built on Apache Lucene, this feature integrates seamlessly with other Elasticsearch functions, including filtering and hybrid search with BM25. However, Elasticsearch's complexity may pose setup and configuration challenges for some users. Lucene's `dense_vector` data type limitations also apply to Elasticsearch, and while it can handle massive vector datasets (in the billions), the memory requirements for ANN at such scales may be impractical.

Each of these vector databases has its unique strengths and weaknesses, depending on the specific use case and requirements. Pinecone excels in ease of use and maintenance, Vespa offers versatility with support for multiple search modalities, Milvus is designed for high performance and scalability, and Weaviate focuses on semantic search with natural language capabilities. Finally, Elasticsearch provides support for dense vectors and ANN search with seamless integration of its search features.

When selecting a vector database, developers should carefully consider their specific needs and evaluate each solution based on its features, performance, and ease of use.

Use cases and domains of application

AI-based search is often overwhelming for a majority of users to get started with, mainly, we believe, because of the lack of standardization – there are a lot of options to get started. In this book, we believe that it would be useful for practitioners to understand where to start by targeting the more mature and adopted techniques, use cases, and domains of application.

We will directly address the scope of possibilities for search, navigating around the jargon carried by the complex space of ML, NLP, and deep learning.

In addition, there is something to keep in mind before jumping into such a project: maintaining a balance between complexity, effort, and cost. By knowing how rapidly the field evolves with new research techniques, the initial investment can be short-lived. In this section, we are going to look at what AI-based search is and also explore the different techniques, such as **named entity recognition** (**NER**), sentiment analysis, text classification, **question-answering** (**QA**), and text summarization with real-life examples you can run.

AI-based search

For the past three years, different industries have been looking for a way to upgrade their customer-facing search experience from a keyword search to a semantic search. In addition to letting the user search as they think, organizations have been looking for paths to personalize their customer experiences based on their browsing behavior.

As discussed previously, full-fledged solutions for this challenge are rare; because the space is so vibrant and rapidly changing, customers often use a privileged platform such as Elastic as it offers them a higher level of flexibility.

Looking at the overall process of building an AI-based search experience can offer perspective on the potential challenge relative to skills, effort, and cost. There are generally five high-level steps for running such a project; we will delve into these in the following subsections:

1. Collecting data
2. Representing the data
3. Applying ML
4. Integrating personalization
5. Getting the project into production

Let's get started.

Collecting data

The first step is probably the most challenging since it is going to provide a universe of known interesting events that will set the boundaries as to what the model is going to be able to learn from. It's about collecting and processing a large enough amount of data for the domain the application is built for. Organizations would use text such as their product descriptions, user-related data, reviews, and even customer support data. The purpose is to train the data for comparison and retrieval.

Representing data

It's one thing to train the data, but it's another to represent it in a mode that would be beneficial to the user experience. Representing the data as vectors in a high-dimensional space using word embeddings or other vectorization techniques is the most effective method at the time of writing. The main benefit is that the vector captures the semantic meaning and the context as well, which ultimately serves the end user experience.

If you're curious, in the situation where an e-commerce customer would search for "wireless headphones," the organization would represent user queries as vectors in a high-dimensional space and use a pre-trained model such as *word2vec* to convert each word in the query into a vector representation. The combined result would represent the entire query. This enables us to compare the vector to the vector space built out of the product representation. The following is a 10-dimensional vector that gives us an idea of the representation:

```
[0.213, -0.178, 0.425, -0.067, 0.321, 0.195, -0.267, 0.132, -0.455,
 -0.033]
```

What's interesting here is the fact that the query is suddenly converted into a space of possibility, which allows us to compare vector space, instead of keywords, to determine similarities. Does the product exist? What type of product is being searched for? The semantics that are extracted from a query are fascinating.

Applying ML

Another level of AI-based search experience is training the data with models such as **convolutional neural networks (CNNs)**, **recurrent neural networks (RNNs)**, or **transformers**. This is done on the previously vectorized data to learn and understand patterns and relationships between data. The goal of this phase is to prepare the search application so that it can support NLP.

To continue our example of wireless headphones, using models such as CNNs or RNNs allows us to browse the graph of connections this specific article could have. In this case, think about features such as noise cancellation, battery life, whether they're waterproof, or whether they stay in the wearer's ears during their burpee session.

Integrating personalization

Without personalization, the search, whether smarter than a keyword search or not, would stay cold. Personalization allows you to integrate context into the search based on past searches and similar searches. These are known as network profiling and user profiling, respectively.

The beauty of CNNs/RNNs/transformers is that the benefits don't stop at what we mentioned previously – they help provide recommendations to users based on their past searches.

Getting into production

We would love to tell you that AI-based search is solving the back and forth that a search application requires from a continuous optimization perspective between relevancy and latency performance, but that's not the case.

The key to having the right data is to make the right decision and limit the optimization effort, which means that not only do you need to be able to fully monitor the user experience, but you also need "interesting events" that let you understand the search quality.

You will need some level of A/B testing for that and compare the performance of a given state to a new state of the search engine, such as after tuning the model. However, you will also need some sort of feedback loop to understand the pertinence of the results.

Once you have built an AI-based search system using the high-level steps I mentioned earlier, you can further enhance the system by incorporating techniques such as NER, sentiment analysis, text classification, Q/A, and text summarization. We'll learn more about these techniques next.

Named Entity Recognition (NER)

NER is a component of NLP that detects and classifies named entities within unstructured text. Entities can be names, brands, locations, or organizations that have a unique name or identifier.

With this technique in place, the unstructured data flowing into the system is classified, which is typically the result of an ML model that's been upstream-trained on annotated data. In this process, the data is labeled with the corresponding type. Once trained, the ML model uses the labels to learn patterns and relationships in the text, allowing it to accurately identify and categorize named entities in new, unseen text.

One of the use cases we can think about is **personally identifiable information** (**PII**), which refers to sensitive information flowing into the system without any control. This information can be names, addresses, social security numbers, and financial information.

For a bank, being unable to detect PII flowing into its data could have serious consequences for both the bank and its customers. For example, if a hacker manages to gain access to the bank's data and steals PII, they can use it to commit fraud and identity theft, which could result in financial losses for customers and penalties for the bank since they are subject to regulations.

That is why financial services companies use NER to mitigate the risk of PII exposure, employing it either on stale data or inflight data during processing. The result is redacting, encrypting, masking, or setting the right privilege to access the data, thus avoiding the legal and reputational risks associated with PII exposure.

Sentiment analysis

Another technique of NLP is sentiment analysis, which aims to identify and extract the sentiment in an unstructured text in terms of emotion. It's commonly used in social networks, such as for extracting emotions from tweets. Often, organizations use it to understand what sentiment relates to their brand.

However, while the usage of sentiment analysis is broad, it is also useful for much more targeted use cases such as analyzing product reviews in real time or monitoring the market sentiment relative to new investments. This helps financial analysts make more informed investments.

The worst that can happen to a company today is failing to detect negative sentiment toward their products or services, which could lead them to suffer reputational damage and customer churn.

The natural language Python toolkit (`https://www.nltk.org/`) comes in handy for this very popular task. The following code example shows how to implement a very simple sentiment analysis and what the results could be:

```
import nltk
nltk.download('vader_lexicon')

from nltk.sentiment import SentimentIntensityAnalyzer
sia = SentimentIntensityAnalyzer()
text = "I really enjoyed the new movie. The acting was great and the
plot was engaging."
scores = sia.polarity_scores(text)
print(scores)
```

You can find the preceding code and run it in this notebook: `https://github.com/PacktPublishing/Vector-Search-for-Practitioners-with-Elastic/blob/main/chapter1/sentiment-analysis.ipynb`. The Python code uses `SentimentIntensityAnalyzer` to perform the actual sentiment analysis. The polarity score is then returned with a score for each polarity (negative, neutral, and positive), as well as a compound score that goes from –1 (most negative) to +1 (most positive). Running the notebook should give you the following result:

```
{'neg': 0.0, 'neu': 0.522, 'pos': 0.478, 'compound': 0.8777}
```

The score states that the emotion that was captured in the text is very positive!

Text classification

Text classification is another NLP technique that assigns predefined categories to unstructured data. A real-life example that affects us all is spam management or the action of filtering and tagging emails as spam or non-spam.

Spam emails can have many signals that would make them suspicious, such as the use of certain keywords, typos, links, and more. Once a model has been trained on a large dataset of labels, emails are classified as spam or non-spam automatically. Multiple values result from this, such as an overall better email experience or increased productivity.

For the sake of simplification, here is an example that uses an online data source and shows classification results, alongside its accuracy:

```
from sklearn.datasets import fetch_20newsgroups
from sklearn.feature_extraction.text import CountVectorizer
from sklearn.naive_bayes import MultinomialNB
from sklearn.metrics import accuracy_score
# Load the dataset
newsgroups_train = fetch_20newsgroups(subset='train')
newsgroups_test = fetch_20newsgroups(subset='test')
# Vectorize the text data
vectorizer = CountVectorizer()
X_train = vectorizer.fit_transform(newsgroups_train.data)
X_test = vectorizer.transform(newsgroups_test.data)
# Train a Naive Bayes classifierclf = MultinomialNB()
clf.fit(X_train, newsgroups_train.target)

# Predict on the test sety_pred = clf.predict(X_test)
# Print the accuracy and predicted classes
print(f"Accuracy: {accuracy_score(newsgroups_test.target, y_pred)}")
print(f"Predicted classes: {y_pred}")
```

Executing the code in a Google Colab notebook should give you the following output:

```
Accuracy: 0.7728359001593202
Predicted classes: [ 7 11 0 ... 9 3 15]
```

Let's understand what we are achieving in the preceding code:

- As we mentioned previously, the code uses an online dataset called the 20 Newsgroup dataset (http://qwone.com/~jason/20Newsgroups/). It's a great playground to test this type of classification as it regroups 20,000 newsgroup documents, partitioned into about 20 different newsgroups. This dataset was assembled by Ken Lang at Carnegie Mellon University.

- We use scikit-learn, better known as sklearn, a very popular and adopted open source ML library for Python. Because it provides a wide range of supervised and unsupervised learning algorithms such as classification, regression, clustering, and dimensionality reduction, we will use it as a tool in this book.

- We use a vector of word count techniques in this example via the CountVectorizer function, which essentially converts text data into a numeric format that can be used for ML.

- We train a naïve Bayes classifier on the vectorized training data. In this example, the classifier assumes that the frequency of each word in a document is independent of the frequency of all other words in the document. The assumption is to make predictions about the class of new documents.

The result is a prediction of the class labels of the test data. Since we used the 20 Newsgroup dataset, the predicted class label is an integer between 0 and 19 to represent the 20 different categories. As an example, the first class label in the array is 7, which means the first instance in the test set belongs to the newsgroup category represented by integer 7. The integer labels are arbitrary here – they don't have any inherent meaning.

Question-answering (QA)

QA became extremely popular at the end of 2022 with the introduction of ChatGPT. Not only does ChatGPT understand the context of the conversation, but it can generate responses that are relevant to the user's question. It is pre-trained on QA models based on the GPT-3 architecture.

QA is a field of NLP that relies on building systems to automatically answer questions posed by humans. It is a very challenging field because, as we mentioned earlier, the system has to understand the context within the scope of the question. Also, questions could be part of a conversation, and multiple conversations can be intertwined in a given session.

Before the introduction of **large language models** (**LLMs**), the process of answering questions in a fact-based QA system required couple of steps:

1. First, the system needed to understand the question and break down the constituent parts into subject, object, and predicate.

2. Then, it needed to rely on a substantial database to search for relevant information and extract and synthesize the answer from the retrieved information.

This process heavily involves text processing, search, and ML algorithms such as deep learning and neural networks.

Let's switch gears and look at this in terms of real life. The healthcare industry is probably an unexpected but good pick. It could essentially assist doctors in providing better patient care. For example, when a doctor has a patient with a complex health background and has to navigate the consequences of prescribing a specific medicine compared to another, a QA system can be of great assistance. Serious side effects can occur with the wrong prescription, and this technique can save time and pain for the patient and provide a better overall quality of service for the healthcare professional or organization.

The following example shows how to use a pre-trained model from the Hugging Face Transformers library to answer a question based on a given context:

```
!pip install transformers
from transformers import pipeline
# Load the question answering model
model = pipeline("question-answering", model="distilbert-base-cased-
distilled-squad", tokenizer="distilbert-base-cased")
# Define a question and a context
question = "What is the capital city of Japan?"
```

```
context = "Japan is an island country in East Asia. Located in the
Pacific Ocean, it lies to the east of the Sea of Japan, China, North
Korea, South Korea and Russia, stretching from the Sea of Okhotsk in
the north to the East China Sea and Taiwan in the south. The capital
city of Japan is Tokyo."
# Get the answer
result = model(question=question, context=context)
# Print the answer
print(f"Answer: {result['answer']}")
```

Here, we load a pre-trained QA model from the `transformers` package and use the `distilbert-base-cased-distilled-squad` model, which is pre-trained on the **Stanford Question Answering Dataset**, better known as **SQuAD**. You can find the dataset at `https://rajpurkar.github.io/SQuAD-explorer/` (credit to Pranav Rajpurkar, Robin Jia, and Percy Liang. 2018. *Know What You Don't Know: Unanswerable Questions for SQuAD*. ArXiv).

We defined a question and a context to answer the question, which we then passed to the model.

If you run the code in a Google Colab notebook, you should get the following output for our question about Japan's capital:

```
Answer: Tokyo
```

Text summarization

Text summarization is another challenging NLP task as it requires understanding the semantics of the document and identifying the most relevant information to keep. We must reduce the information in text without losing its meaning and accuracy.

One real-life example we are all used to is the new feeds we consume daily. The application you use to consume this summarizes data to gain your attention. There is a real challenge in this process as the news feed industry has the constraint of living in a real-time environment where any nanoseconds of your scrolling experience matter. In this short window of time when you see a given piece of news, the summary should incentivize you to tap and get onto the news page, which almost certainly contains a lot of ads that are key to the press agencies gaining revenue.

The following example uses the Hugging Face Transformers library to summarize a blob of text from `https://en.wikipedia.org/wiki/Blue-throated_macaw`:

```
!pip install transformers
from transformers import pipeline
# Define the text to be summarized
text = "The blue-throated macaw (Ara glaucogularis) is a species of
macaw that is endemic to a small area of north-central Bolivia, known
as the Llanos de Moxos. Recent population and range estimates suggest
that about 350 to 400 individuals remain in the wild. Its demise was
brought on by nesting competition, avian predation, and a small native
```

```
range, exacerbated by indigenous hunting and capture for the pet
trade. Although plentiful in captivity, it is critically endangered in
the wild and protected by trading prohibitions. In 2014, the species
was designated a natural patrimony of Bolivia. This blue-throated
macaw in flight was photographed at Loro Parque, on the Spanish island
of Tenerife in the Canary Islands."
# Instantiate the summarization pipeline
summarizer = pipeline("summarization")
# Generate a summary of the text
summary = summarizer(text, max_length=100, min_length=30, do_
sample=False)[0]["summary_text"]
# Print the summary
print(summary)
```

Using `summarizer` and the `DistilBert` model from Hugging Face and passing parameters such as the maximum and minimum length give us the following output:

```
The blue-throated macaw (Ara glaucogularis) is a species of macaw that
is endemic to a small area of north-central Bolivia, known as the
Llanos de Moxos . Recent population and range estimates suggest that
about 350 to 400 individuals remain in the wild .
```

The number of models available at your fingertips is quite impressive. Communities such as Hugging Face accelerate your productivity by enabling you to run complex NLP tasks without having to even fine-tune a model.

At this point, you should have a good grasp of AI-based search, a good understanding of how to use the available techniques, and even be able to integrate some of your learning immediately into the code of your application.

How is Elastic playing a role in this space?

Now, what role does Elastic play here? There are multiple ways you can leverage Elastic – including Elasticsearch. Elasticsearch is a distributed and highly scalable data store. Its specialty is information retrieval. It's one thing to run the preceding code in a notebook – it's another to make it operational at scale and to be accessed by hundreds, thousands, or millions of users.

Furthermore, training can be long as it requires the algorithm to be able to access a large amount of data, indexed for fast access, at scale. There are very few data stores that are versatile enough to be able to cope with structured and unstructured data at the same time, manage a wide range of data types, and be scalable for ingestion and search.

Elasticsearch is a unique choice, not only because of its technical attributes but also because of its vibrant community and large adoption. As mentioned earlier, the field of AI-based search applications is rapidly changing, so some consistency along the way is a luxury. Technology and communities such as Elasticsearch and Hugging Face allow users to have a safety net and some resiliency against change in the process.

We like to describe Elasticsearch as a search and analytics engine. The analytics side of Elasticsearch plays a crucial role as it allows you to perform complex queries and aggregation on data.

However, the icing on the cake is Elasticsearch's extensibility. In 2021, Elastic introduced the capability to index vectors. This means that Elasticsearch natively understands what a vector is and is optimized for the task, not letting users manage and force the data store to handle non-supported data types.

Beyond search, we would like to open your mind and see how we could apply vector search to other use cases, such as observability and cybersecurity.

A primer on observability and cybersecurity

Vectors are not only important for tasks such as NLP but also important in fields such as observability and cybersecurity. They allow for efficient processing and analysis of large volumes of data.

Let's pause for a second and think about the current state of observability. Today, operations teams have several tools in their toolbelt to accelerate the investigation process, such as anomaly detection, while mainly relying on unsupervised learning. Now, text classification could be a great benefit for signals such as logs, where the data is fairly unstructured and needs to be grouped into buckets. The outcome is a better analyst experience and accelerated root cause analysis. Now, let's think about what a future state would look like. By vectorizing data – in other words, converting data points into vectors – it becomes much easier to identify patterns and anomalies.

In cybersecurity, vectors can be used to represent and analyze multiple types of data, such as network traffic, malware signatures, and user behavior.

We will address observability and cybersecurity in *Chapters 7* and *8*, respectively, and look at practical examples you can use and apply in your environment, after which we will extend them to other places where we see fit.

Summary

This book is going to guide you through pragmatic, practical examples that you will be able to replicate for your needs, ranging from building a vector-powered search application to applying vectors to domains such as observability and security. It targets a large spectrum of practitioners but is more focused on the operations teams, which deal with specific challenges and could make good use of combining vectors and Elastic.

In this chapter, you learned about the key aspects of NLP, vector search, AI-based search, and its relative techniques. You were also shown pieces of code that you can run and adapt for your business applications. Lastly, you gained a high-level understanding of Elasticsearch's role in this context as well as how to apply vector search beyond the search use case, such as in terms of observability.

In the next chapter, we will get started by looking at vectors in Elasticsearch. We will explore the current search methodology and see how vectors are augmenting and enhancing it. Furthermore, we will dive deep into the technicality of vector implementation in Elasticsearch.

2

Getting Started with Vector Search in Elastic

Welcome to *Getting Started with Vector Search in Elastic*. In this chapter, we will understand the fundamental paradigm of search with Elastic and how vector search has emerged as a powerful tool for real-time, context-aware, accurate information retrieval.

In this chapter, we are going to cover the following topics:

- Search experience in Elastic before the addition of vector search
- The need for new representations such as vectors and **Hierarchical Navigable Small World (HNSW)**
- A new vector data type
- Different strategies to configure the mapping and challenges of storing vectors, getting a better perspective on how to optimize its implementation
- How to build queries including brute force, **k-nearest neighbors (kNN)**, and exact match as a resource

Whether you are a seasoned Elastic user or just getting started, this chapter will provide valuable insights into the power of vector search in Elastic. Let's begin!

Search experience in Elastic before vectors

Before the introduction of vector search in Elastic, the primary relevancy model was based on text search and analysis capabilities. Elasticsearch provides various data types (https://www.elastic.co/guide/en/elasticsearch/reference/current/mapping-types.html) and analyzers (https://www.elastic.co/guide/en/elasticsearch/reference/current/analysis-analyzers.html) to provide efficient search. In this part, we will level-set and make sure we all have an understanding of what the "before state" looks like.

Data type and its impact on relevancy

There are various data types in Elasticsearch, but for the purpose of this part, it wouldn't be useful to go through them one by one. Instead, we will divide them into two categories: the type that directly drives the relevancy ranking and the types that indirectly influence the ranking. The goal is to understand how they are related to relevancy models.

The first type that we will look at is one that directly impacts relevancy ranking:

- **Text**: The `text` data type is the most crucial data type for the relevancy model in Elasticsearch. It is used to store and search textual data such as articles and product descriptions. Text data is analyzed using built-in analyzers, which break the text into tokens and perform operations such as lowercasing, stemming, and filtering.

- **Geo**: The `geo` data type is used to store and search geographic coordinates. It enables you to perform geo-based queries, such as finding documents within a specific distance or bounding box. Although not part of the text-based relevancy model, geo-based queries can help to narrow down search results and improve their relevance.

The second type of data types are ones that improve relevancy:

- **Keyword**: The `keyword` data type is used to store non-analyzed text data, typically used for filtering and aggregations. It helps to refine the search results by applying filters or aggregations, thereby improving the relevance of the results.

- **Numeric types (integer, float, double, etc.)**: These data types are used to store and search numeric data. Although they don't directly impact the text-based relevancy model, they can be used to filter or sort search results, which can indirectly affect the relevancy of the results.

- **Date**: The `date` data type is used to store and search date and time data. Similar to numeric types, date data types can be used to filter and sort search results, impacting the overall relevancy indirectly.

- **Boolean**: The `boolean` data type is used to store `true`/`false` values. While it doesn't
  - contribute directly to the relevancy model, it can be used to filter search results, improving their relevance.

The relevancy model

While this book is not an Elasticsearch cookbook and focuses on vector search, it is important to understand relevancy ranking models before diving into vectors, so that we can use them wherever required. We will see that building a hybrid search by combining vector search and "traditional" search is a technique that will improve the end user experience.

Elasticsearch itself went through iteration when it comes to the relevancy model, first with **term frequency-inverse document frequency** (**TF-IDF**) and now with BM25. Both are text retrieval algorithms used to rank documents based on their relevance to a query. However, they have key differences, which we will explore now.

TF-IDF

To illustrate the TF-IDF concept, we will use a simple example with a small collection of three documents:

- **Document 1**: "I love vector search. Vector search is amazing."
- **Document 2**: "Vector search is a method for searching high-dimensional data."
- **Document 3**: "Elasticsearch is a powerful search engine that supports vector search."

We want to calculate the TF-IDF score for the term vector search in each document.

First, we calculate the **term frequency** (**TF**) for each document; note that we apply TF on a **bi-gram** (a sequence of two adjacent words in a text – i.e., vector and search together) here:

Document 1: vector search appears twice out of 8 words: TF = 2 / 8 = **0.25**

Document 2: vector search appears once out of 9 words: TF = 1 / 9 = **0.111**

Document 3: vector search appears once out of 10 words: TF = 1 / 10 = **0.110**

Then, we calculate the **inverse document frequency** (**IDF**) for the term vector search.

We know that the number of documents containing the term vector search = 3.

And the total number of documents = 3.

When these are used in the formula, we get:

$$IDF \ = \ log\left(\tfrac{3}{3}\right) = log(1) = 0$$

Finally, we calculate the TF-IDF score for the term vector search in each document:

- **Document 1**: TF-IDF = TF * IDF = 0.25 * 0 = 0
- **Document 2**: TF-IDF = TF * IDF = 0.111 * 0 = 0
- **Document 3**: TF-IDF = TF * IDF = 0.110 * 0 = 0

In this specific example, the IDF value is 0 because the term vector search appears in all documents, making it a common term across the entire document collection. As a result, the TF-IDF scores for all documents are also 0. This illustrates how the IDF component in the TF-IDF algorithm penalizes common terms in the document collection, reducing their impact on the relevance scores.

By modifying the third document to "Elasticsearch is a powerful search engine that supports semantic search.", searching for `semantic search`, and applying what we just learned, the ranking becomes the following:

- Document 3 (TF-IDF = **0.109**)
- Document 1 (TF-IDF = **0**)
- Document 2 (TF-IDF = **0**)

While straightforward and simple, this approach can lead to bias with longer documents, since they generally have higher term frequencies. Here are two additional points to consider:

- The IDF component is calculated as `log(N/df(t))`, where N is the total number of documents in the collection, and `df(t)` is the number of documents containing the term t. The IDF component aims to give more importance to rare terms and less importance to common terms.
- The TF has no upper bound, which means that as the frequency of a term increases, its impact on the relevance score also increases linearly.

This leads us to consider the following method to rank the documents.

BM25

With BM25, Elasticsearch is able to increase fidelity to data and refine the TF and IDF components of the equation. For example, BM25 introduces a saturation component, which means that the impact of a term on the relevance score levels off at a certain point, even if its frequency in the document continues to increase. This saturation prevents extremely high-term frequencies from dominating the relevance score.

The following chart shows how TF-IDF keeps increasing with frequency, whereas BM25 neutralizes it:

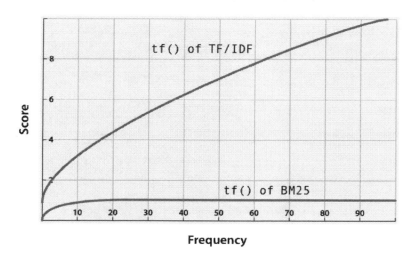

Figure 2.1: The TF-IDF and BM25 scores by frequency comparison

You can find out more info at this blog post:

`https://www.elastic.co/blog/practical-bm25-part-2-the-bm25-algorithm-and-its-variables`

For the sake of simplicity and to illustrate the benefit of BM25, we will go through a similar example as we previously did for TF-IDF.

We will use the same documents as before, but now, we will calculate the BM25 score for the term `search`. The goal is to highlight the benefits of BM25, such as term frequency normalization and saturation:

- **Document 1**: "I love vector search. Vector search is amazing."

- **Document 2**: "Vector search is a method for searching high-dimensional data."

- **Document 3**: "Elasticsearch is a powerful search engine that supports semantic search."

First, we calculate the TF for each document:

- **Document 1**: `search` appears 2 times out of 8 words: TF= 2 / 8 = **0.25**

- **Document 2**: `search` appears 2 times out of 9 words: TF = 1 / 9 = **0.111**

- **Document 3**: `search` appears 2 times out of 9 words: TF = 2 / 10 = **0.2**

Now, we will calculate the BM25 score for each document using the following formula:

$$\sum_{i}^{n} IDF(q_i) = \frac{f(q_i, D) \cdot (k1 + 1)}{f(q_i, D) + k1 \cdot \left(1 - b + b \cdot \frac{fieldLen}{avgFieldLen}\right)}$$

First, let's take a look at how to calculate the TF normalization and then the IDF.

TF normalization

Let's assume that k1 = 1.2 and b = 0.75. The **average document length** (**avgdl**) is (8 + 9 + 9) / 3 = 8.666:

- **Document 1**: ((1.2 + 1) * 2) / (1.2 * (1 - 0.75 + 0.75 * (8 / 8.666)) + 2) = **1.405**

- **Document 2**: ((1.2 + 1) * 2) / (1.2 * (1 - 0.75 + 0.75 * (9 / 8.666)) + 2) = **1.360**

- **Document 3**: ((1.2 + 1) * 2) / (1.2 * (1 - 0.75 + 0.75 * (10 / 8.666)) + 2) = **1.317**

IDF

The IDF component in BM25 is calculated as `log((N-df(t)+0.5)/(df(t) +0.5))`, where `N` is the total number of documents and `df(t)` is the number of documents containing the term `t`.

As we know, the number of documents containing the term `search` = **3**.

And the total number of documents = **3**. So, we have the following:

IDF = log((3 - 3 + 0.5) / (3 + 0.5)) ≈ **0.287** (using the natural logarithm)

BM25 score

- **Document 1**: BM25 = IDF * TF normalization = 0.287 * **1.405≈0.403**

- **Document 2**: BM25 = IDF * TF normalization = 0.287 * **1.360≈0.390**

- **Document 3**: BM25 = IDF * TF normalization = 0.287 * **1.317≈ 0.377**

Based on the BM25 scores, we can rank the documents for the query search as follows:

- **Document 2** (BM25 = **0.403**)

- **Document 1** (BM25 = **0.390**)

- **Document 3** (BM25 = **0.377**)

This demonstrates one of the benefits of BM25, its ability to handle efficiently versatile document lengths than TF-IDF. The normalization helps reduce the bias toward longer documents, which have higher term frequencies because they have more words.

We haven't shown here that BM25 presents extremely high term frequencies from dominating the relevance score, but if you play with more complex scenarios, you will see the difference illustrated in *Figure 2.1*, where high term frequency doesn't receive an unjustly high relevance score.

At this stage, you should have a solid understanding of TF-IDF and, more specifically, BM25. The topics covered so far will not only assist you in the remainder of this chapter in understanding the differences between keyword-based search and vector search (with a significant one being calculating the relevance of search) but also prove beneficial in later stages of this book, during the discussion on hybrid search.

Evolution of search experience

We are now going to see how users' demand for a better search experience requires us to consider other techniques than just keyword-based search. In this section, we will approach the limitations of keyword-based search, understand what vector representation entails, and how the meta representation HNSW emerged to facilitate information retrieval with vector.

The limits of keyword-based search

For those of you who are comparatively new to the subject matter, before we talk about vector representation, we need to understand why the industry and keyword-based search experience have reached their limits, failing to fully meet end-user requirements.

Keyword-based search relies on exact matches between the user query and the terms contained in documents, which could lead to missed relevant results if the search system is not refined enough with synonyms, abbreviations, alternative phrasings, and so on. Therefore, it is important for the search system to relate given words with other words that are part of the same semantic space.

As keyword-based searches lack context understanding, they don't consider the context or meaning of words. Therefore, clarifying the context of a word is important. For example, the word "bat" is a word with different meanings in different contexts – in a sports context, a "bat" can refer to the bat used in baseball or cricket to hit a ball. In a zoological context, a "bat" refers to a flying mammal.

Individual words can already be challenging because of the preceding limitation, and you can add to this language dependence, typos, and spelling variations. Furthermore, keyword-based search does not capture the structure or semantics of sentences. For instance, how words are sequenced in a query can be important to understand its meaning. The order of words can be important to understand the meaning of a query. There is a semantic relationship between terms, which makes it difficult to retrieve documents that discuss the same topic using different vocabulary.

A good example of the limitation of keyword-based search due to the lack of semantic understanding can be seen in a search query related to the topic of "global warming."

Suppose a user searches for documents using the term "global warming," but some relevant documents use the term "climate change" instead of "global warming." Since keyword-based search doesn't capture the semantic relationship between "global warming" and "climate change," it may not retrieve relevant documents that discuss the same topic using different vocabulary.

To be clear, there are techniques out there to cope with the aforementioned limitations, but they hardly scale or are hard to maintain, and require a decent amount of expertise. Instead, models when used to generate embedding can help address many of the limitations of keyword-based search.

Vector representation

As explained in *Chapter 1, Introduction to Vectors and Embeddings*, a vector representation is a way to convert complex data such as text into a fixed-size numerical format that can be easily processed by machine learning processes. In natural language processing, it helps to capture the semantic meaning of words, sentences, and documents, making it easier to perform tasks as described in *Chapter 1*. We will now look into the vectorization process of taking raw data, extracting the feature, and converting it into a number representation using a model. Furthermore, we will familiarize ourselves with HNSW and its role in the search process.

Vectorization process

From a high-level perspective, the process of building vectors consists of the following steps:

1. First, the text is processed – that is, the raw data is cleaned and preprocessed to remove noise, correct spelling errors, and convert text to a standardized format.

    Common processing steps involve tasks such as **lowercasing, tokenization, stopword removal, stemming**, and **lemmatization**. It is very close, not to say similar, to what Elastic does when sending and indexing data with tasks executed before indexation happens with analyzers. Note that this could hurt the embedding models because semantic nuances could be removed by these data processes.

2. After preprocessing the data, the relevant features are extracted from the text. This can be done using techniques such as **Bag-of-Words (BoW)**, TF-IDF, or more advanced techniques such as **word embeddings**.

    Word embeddings are dense vector representations that capture the semantic meaning of words in a continuous vector space. Dense vector representations, unlike sparse representations such as BoW or TF-IDF where most of the values are zeros, have non-zero values in most dimensions. This means that word embeddings store more information in a smaller space, making them more efficient and computationally manageable. Word embeddings map words to points in a continuous multidimensional space. This means that the position of each word in the space is determined by a continuous set of numerical values (the word's vector), and the distances between words in the space can be measured using various distance metrics, such as Euclidean or cosine distance. A continuous vector space allows smooth transitions between related words, making it easier to identify and manipulate semantic relationships.

3. Once the features are extracted, they can be converted to numerical vectors that can be used as input for machine learning processes. Each dimension of the vector corresponds to a specific feature, and the value in that dimension reflects the importance or relevance of that feature in the given text.

In conjunction with vector representations, algorithms can be used to perform approximate nearest neighbor searches in high-dimensional spaces, which is the goal of HNSW.

HNSW

You can find the initial paper about HNSW on the Cornell University website `https://arxiv.org/abs/1603.09320`, but here, we are going to break it down into multiple fundamental parts to get a good take on what it is and what it achieves.

As mentioned previously, an algorithm is required to perform a nearest neighbor search in a high-dimensional space. The HNSW algorithm can help quickly find similar texts based on their vector representations.

From a high-level perspective, HNSW constructs a hierarchical graph where each node is mapped to a text's vector representation. The graph is built in a way that it has small-world properties, allowing efficient search in high-dimensional spaces, as shown in the following diagram:

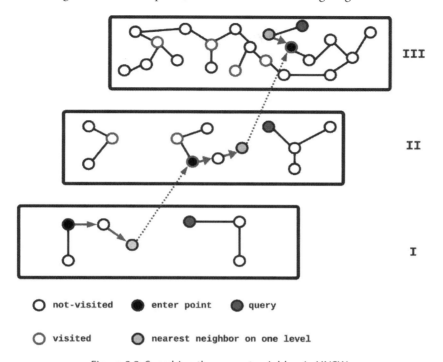

Figure 2.2: Searching the nearest neighbor in HNSW

Then, the approximate nearest neighbor search finds similar texts to a given query text. The query is first converted into a vector representation, using the same method used for the dataset so that the nearest vector representation to the query is found in the vector space.

HNSW is based on the idea of "small-world" networks. In a small-world network, most nodes are not neighbors but can be reached from any other node in a small number of hops.

When searching for the nearest neighbor in high-dimensional spaces, traditional methods can get stuck in local minima. Imagine climbing a mountain and trying to reach the highest peak, but you end up on a smaller peak nearby because it's the highest point you can see from where you're standing. That's a local minimum.

HNSW overcomes this by maintaining multiple levels (layers) of the graph. When searching, HNSW starts at the top layer, which has fewer nodes as compared to the deeper layers, and covers a broader area; thus, it is less likely to get stuck in local minima. It then works its way down, refining the search as it goes deeper until it reaches the base layer, which has the detailed data.

The search stops when the algorithm finds a node that is closer to the query than any other node in its neighborhood. At this point, it's believed to have found the closest (or approximately closest) match in the dataset, based on the layer it's currently searching.

There are several reasons for HNSW's popularity:

- **Efficiency**: It provides a balance between accuracy and speed. While it's an approximate method, its accuracy is often good enough for many applications.

- **Memory usage**: It's more memory-efficient than some other approximate nearest neighbor methods.

- **Versatility**: It's not tied to a specific distance metric. It can work with Euclidean, cosine, and other distance measures.

Here, each layer is a subset of nodes from the previous layer. The bottom layer contains all the nodes, which is the vector representation of the texts. The top layer has fewer nodes that act as the entry points for the search process. Each node is connected to its k nearest neighbors, based on a distance metric such as Euclidean, dot product, or cosine distance.

Now that you understand the concept behind HNSW, let's take a look at how to calculate distances.

Distance metric

Because Elasticsearch offers the three distance evaluation methods as choices, this is how to calculate them:

- **Euclidean distance**:

  $d(A, B) = \sqrt{\left((A_1 - B_1)^2 + (A_2 - B_2)^2 + \ldots + (A_n - B_n)^2\right)}$, where $d(A,B)$ is the Euclidean distance. In a 2D plan, it's simply the length of the line connecting points A to B.

- **Dot product**:

  $$a.b = \sum_{i=1}^{n} a_i b_i = a_1 b_1 + a_2 b_2 + \ldots + a_n b_n$$

  Here, $a.b$ is the dot product.

  Geometrically, if there is angle θ between a and b, then $a \cdot b = |a|\,|b|\,cos(\theta)$, as represented here:

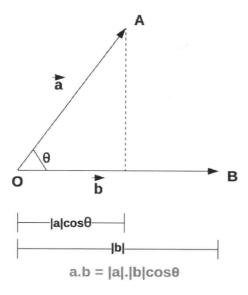

Figure 2.3: Dot product

- |a| = magnitude (or length) of vector a

- |b| = magnitude (or length) of vector b

- cos(θ) = cosine of the angle between the vectors

Here is an example, in the context of vector search, for 2 vectors A and B:

- A could represent a document about "machine learning."

- B represents a document about "deep learning."

- Given the close relationship between "machine learning" and "deep learning," we expect these vectors to be somewhat close in the vector space, but not identical. This means they would have a relatively small angle between them.

- **Cosine similarity**:

$S_c(A,B) = \frac{(A \cdot B)}{(\|A\| \cdot \|B\|)}$, where $S_c(A,B)$ is the cosine similarity.

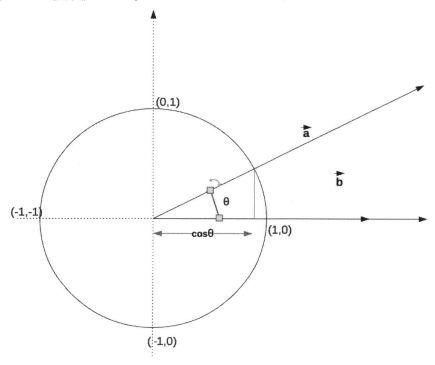

Figure 2.4: Cosine similarity

For vectors A, B with values such as: A = [1, 2] B = [3, 4], their distances would be as follows:

- `Euclidean_distance` ≈ 2.83

- `Dot_product` = 11

- `Cosine_similarity` ≈ 0.98

The question you might have is when to choose one or the other. The answer depends on the use case, the text that has been vectorized, the domain, and the vector space shape.

The Euclidean distance, for example, is used when working with data that has a meaningful origin. In a 2D cartesian coordinate system, the origin refers to the zero point, (0,0). A meaningful origin carries some significance or meaning in the context of the data being analyzed. In other words, a meaningful origin is a point at which all feature values are zero and has a distinct interpretation in the problem domain. A good example I can think of is when measuring temperature in degrees; the origin (0°C) represents the freezing point of water under normal atmospheric pressure. This origin has a specific, meaningful interpretation in the context of temperature measurement.

The dot product is interesting when working with data that has both positive and negative values, and where the angle between vectors is not important. Dot product can be positive, negative, or zero. It is not normalized, so the magnitudes of the vectors can impact the results. In addition, if the vectors are normalized (i.e., their magnitudes are 1), the cosine similarity of normalized vectors is equivalent to the dot product:

$$\cos similarity = A.B = dot\ product$$

This is valuable information, as vector search on Elasticsearch is faster with the dot product.

In the context of a vector representing text, vectors can have both negative and positive values. These values are derived from the training process and the algorithms used to create the embeddings. The positive or negative values in these vectors do not necessarily have a specific meaning by themselves. So, two vectors with high magnitudes but very different directions will have a large dot product, even though they are not semantically similar.

In contrast, cosine similarity, derived from the dot product, normalizes the magnitude of vectors and focuses on the angle between them, which makes them much more suitable for text data. It measures the cosine of the angle between vectors, capturing their semantic similarity. Since it's normalized, ranging from −1 to 1, cosine similarity that is less sensitive to the scale of the features is also less sensitive to the magnitude.

Note the two important components to understand here:

- The direction which is defined by the angle between vectors
- The magnitude

Let's look at these components in detail.

Directions and magnitude

We have seen that, in the context of text data, vectors are typically created using word embeddings or document embeddings, which are dense vector representations that capture the semantic meaning of words or documents in a continuous vector space.

The direction and magnitude of these vectors are related to the actual text through the relationship between words in the dataset. The direction of a vector representation of text indicates the semantic orientation of the text in the high-dimensional vector space. Vectors with similar directions represent semantically similar texts. They share similar context or meanings. In other words, the angle between the vectors of two texts is small when the texts are semantically related.

In contrast, if the angle is large, it indicates that the texts have different meanings or contexts. This is why cosine similarity, which focuses on the angle between vectors, is a popular choice to measure semantic similarity in text data.

Here's an example of the direction of a vector, assuming the following samples would have been converted to vector representations using a word embedding technique:

- **A**: "The cat is playing with a toy."

- **B**: "A kitten is interacting with a plaything."

- **C**: "The chef is cooking a delicious meal."

The angle between A and B is likely to be small; they have similar meanings. In contrast, the angle between the vectors representing A and C would certainly be large, given how they are semantically different.

The magnitude of a vector represents the weight of the text in the vector space. In some cases, the magnitude can relate to the frequency of words in the text or the importance of the text in the dataset. However, the magnitude can also be influenced by things such as the length of the text or the presence of certain words, which might be indicative of semantic similarities.

Here's another example:

- **D**: "Economics is the social science that studies the production, distribution, and consumption of goods and services."

- **E**: "Economics studies goods and services."

D is longer and provides a more detailed definition of economics. E is shorter and provides a more concise definition. This difference in length might result in the magnitude of the vector representing D being greater than E. However, the difference does not indicate a difference in semantics. In fact, D and E have similar meanings and should be considered semantically similar, despite their different magnitudes.

When comparing texts in high-dimensional space, the direction is often more important than their magnitudes if the goal is to capture the semantic similarity, since the angle directly represents the similarity between words.

Here is an example of code you can run in Google Collab, which you can find in the `chapter 2` folder of this book's GitHub repository (`https://github.com/PacktPublishing/Vector-Search-for-Practitioners-with-Elastic/tree/main/chapter2`), to look at the Euclidean distance, cosine similarity, and the magnitude of the vector representations of our text samples. We will use the `spaCy` library to create the vector representation:

```
# Install spaCy and download the 'en_core_web_md' model
!pip install spacy
!python -m spacy download en_core_web_md
import spacy
import numpy as np
from scipy.spatial.distance import cosine, euclidean
```

```
# Load the pre-trained word embeddings model
nlp = spacy.load('en_core_web_md')
# Define the texts
text_a = "The cat is playing with a toy."
text_b = "A kitten is interacting with a plaything."
text_c = "The chef is cooking a delicious meal."
text_d = "Economics is the social science that studies the production,
distribution, and consumption of goods and services."
text_e = "Economics studies goods and services."
# Convert the texts to vector representations using the spaCy model
vector_a = nlp(text_a).vector
vector_b = nlp(text_b).vector
vector_c = nlp(text_c).vector
vector_d = nlp(text_d).vector
vector_e = nlp(text_e).vector
 # Calculate the cosine similarity between the vectors
cosine_sim_ab = 1 - cosine(vector_a, vector_b)
cosine_sim_ac = 1 - cosine(vector_a, vector_c)
cosine_sim_de = 1 - cosine(vector_d, vector_e)
print(f"Cosine similarity between Text A and Text B: {cosine_sim_
ab:.2f}")
print(f"Cosine similarity between Text A and Text C: {cosine_sim_
ac:.2f}")
print(f"Cosine similarity between Text D and Text E: {cosine_sim_
de:.2f}")
# Calculate the Euclidean distance between the vectors
euclidean_dist_ab = euclidean(vector_a, vector_b)
euclidean_dist_ac = euclidean(vector_a, vector_c)
euclidean_dist_de = euclidean(vector_d, vector_e)
print(f"Euclidean distance between Text A and Text B: {euclidean_dist_
ab:.2f}")
print(f"Euclidean distance between Text A and Text C: {euclidean_dist_
ac:.2f}")
print(f"Euclidean distance between Text D and Text E: {euclidean_dist_
de:.2f}")
# Calculate the magnitudes of the vectors
magnitude_d = np.linalg.norm(vector_d)
magnitude_e = np.linalg.norm(vector_e)
print(f"Magnitude of Text D's vector: {magnitude_d:.2f}")
print(f"Magnitude of Text E's vector: {magnitude_e:.2f}")
```

The output will show you the results of the distance calculation, which will give some perspective on which one to use in this case.

At this stage, you should have a good grasp of some of the fundamental concepts that constitute the vector representation of text, as well as understand how to determine the similarity between these vectors and, thus, the semantic similarities between text. We will now explore Elastic and look at how to put this into practice.

The new vector data type and the vector search query API

At this point of the chapter, you should have a good understanding of relevancy ranking in Elasticsearch and how a vector extends the capabilities of search in domains that keyword-based search couldn't even compete with. We have also covered how vectors are organized into an HNSW graph, stored in memory in Elasticsearch, and the options to evaluate the distance between vectors. Now, we are going to take this knowledge and put it into action by understanding the dense vector data type available in Elasticsearch, setting up our Elastic Cloud environment, and finally, building and running vector search queries.

Sparse and dense vectors

Elasticsearch supports a new data type as part of the mapping called `dense_vector`. It is used to store arrays of numeric values. These arrays are vector representation of text semantic. Ultimately, dense vectors are leveraged in the context of vector search and kNN search.

The documentation for the `dense_vector` type can be found here: `https://www.elastic.co/guide/en/elasticsearch/reference/current/dense-vector.html`.

Sparse vectors are vectors that have few non-zero values, with most of the dimensions having zero values. This results in a low-dimensional vector space, which is more memory-efficient and faster to process than dense vectors.

For example, consider a vocabulary of 100,000 words and a document of 100 words. If we represent the document using dense vectors, we will need to allocate the memory for the 100,000 words, even though most of them would be zeros. In contrast, the same document with sparse vectors would only need the memory for the 100 non-zero values, which is a significant memory usage reduction. The reason is that the dense vector representation of a document or text assigns a non-zero value to every possible word in the vocabulary.

If you want to see an example in action, here is one notebook that builds both sparse and dense vector representations of a text and helps you visually understand through heatmaps the difference between the two:

```
import numpy as np
from scipy.sparse import random
from sklearn.decomposition import TruncatedSVD
import matplotlib.pyplot as plt

# Generate a corpus of 100 documents, each containing 1000 words
```

```
vocab_size = 10000
num_docs = 100
doc_len = 1000

# Create a vocabulary of 10000 words
vocab = [f'word{i}' for i in range(vocab_size)]

# Generate a random dense vector representing each document
dense_vectors = np.zeros((num_docs, vocab_size))
for i in range(num_docs):
    word_indices = np.random.choice(vocab_size, doc_len)
    for j in word_indices:
        dense_vectors[i, j] += 1

# Convert Create the dense vectors to sparse format
sparse_vectors = random(num_docs, vocab_size, density=0.01,
format='csr')
for i in range(num_docs):
    word_indices = np.random.choice(vocab_size, doc_len)
    for j in word_indices:
        sparse_vectors[i, j] += 1

# Use TruncatedSVD to reduce the dimensionality of the dense vectors
svd = TruncatedSVD(n_components=2)
dense_vectors_svd = svd.fit_transform(dense_vectors)

# Apply TruncatedSVD to the sparse vectors
sparse_vectors_svd = svd.transform(sparse_vectors)

# Plot the dense and sparse vectors on a scatter plot
fig, ax = plt.subplots(figsize=(10, 8))
ax.scatter(dense_vectors_svd[:, 0], dense_vectors_svd[:, 1], c='b',
label='Dense vectors')
ax.scatter(sparse_vectors_svd[:, 0], sparse_vectors_svd[:, 1], c='r',
label='Sparse vectors')
ax.set_title('2D embeddings of dense and sparse document vectors after
TruncatedSVD dimensionality reduction')
ax.set_xlabel('Dimension 1')
ax.set_ylabel('Dimension 2')
ax.legend()
plt.show()
```

The preceding example generates a corpus of 100 documents, each containing 1,000 words randomly selected from a vocabulary of 10,000 words. It creates dense and sparse vectors representing each document. The code uses a dimensionality reduction technique through the `TruncatedSVD` function so that it can visualize the vector in 2D. It should take about two minutes to run the code with the default document count, vocabulary size, and document length settings. The results should be close to this:

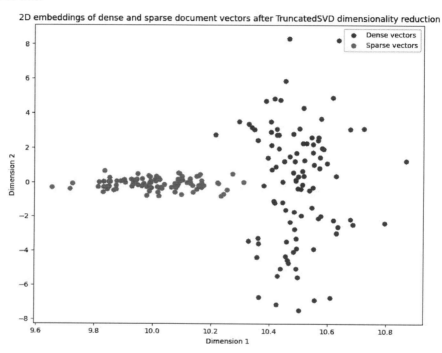

Figure 2.5: A scatter plot of dense and sparse vectors

The scatter plot shows 2D embeddings of document vectors after dimensionality reduction. Dense vectors (right) are spread out, indicating diverse content, while sparse vectors (left) are closely clustered, hinting at similar content. The differences highlight the distinct characteristics of dense and sparse representations in the reduced space.

Sparse vectors are more memory-efficient because they only store non-zero values, while dense vectors allocate memory for every value. The latter is often the preferred choice in deep learning models, as they capture more complex relationships between words in documents since they assign a non-zero value to every word in the vocabulary. The value is assigned based on the frequency and the context in the document. The other advantage of sparse vectors is because they have a fixed size and shape, the values are stored in contiguous memory, making it easier for mathematical operations such as matrix multiplication.

An Elastic Cloud quick start

From now on, you will need a sandbox where you will be able to run the example in this book. You need to have a running Elasticsearch instance and a Kibana instance. The shortest and best path for that is using Elastic Cloud. If you haven't done so yet, sign up at `https://cloud.elastic.co`.

Once done, log in and go ahead and create a new deployment by clicking on the **Create Deployment** button:

Welcome to Elastic Cloud

Dedicated deployments ⑦   Create deployment

Deployment	Status	Version	Cloud provider & region		Actions
apm-cluster	Healthy	8.10.1	AWS - N. Virginia (us-east-1)	Open	Manage
slack-app	Healthy	8.3.0	GCP - Iowa (us-central1)	Open	Manage

Figure 2.6: The Dedicated deployments list and the Create deployment button

Don't forget to download your credentials to connect to your deployment. They appear during the deployment process:

Save the deployment credentials
These root credentials are shown only once.
They provide super user access to your deployment. Keep them safe.

Username
elastic

Password

czkxAnw8PseG6VQDnFHGDioK 📋

Download

Skip

Figure 2.7: Deployment credentials

Once the deployment is created, go back to `https://cloud.elastic.co/deployments` and click on your deployment there:

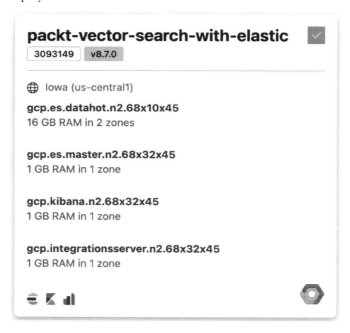

Figure 2.8: A newly created deployment

You will be redirected to the deployment page and see all the useful endpoints there:

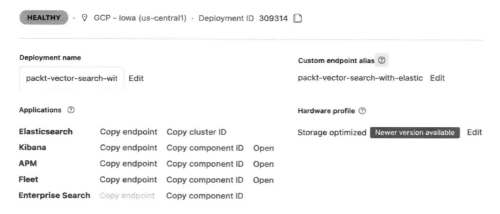

Figure 2.9: The deployment page and endpoint list

In the upcoming exercises, you will mainly need the Elasticsearch endpoint, but you might want to access Kibana to run queries, or for use when we build visualizations.

Dense vector mapping

Now, let's take a look at how to build a mapping in Elasticsearch for dense vectors. It's a straightforward exercise; here is an example of a mapping:

```
{
  "mappings": {
    "properties": {
      "embedding": {
        "type": "dense_vector",
        "dims": 768,
      }
    }
  }
}
```

Simply put, the preceding example defines a field called embedding where the dense vectors will be stored. We set the dimensions as 768 because, in the following example, we use a **BERT model**, bert-base-encased, which has 768 hidden units. The BERT model is a pre-trained deep learning model used for NLP tasks, which processes lowercase text and can understand the context of a word based on its surrounding words:

```
!pip install transformers elasticsearch
import numpy as np
from transformers import AutoTokenizer, AutoModel
from elasticsearch import Elasticsearch
import torch

# Define Elasticsearch connection with credentials
es = Elasticsearch(
        ['https://hostname:port'],
        http_auth=('username', 'password'),
            verify_certs=False
)

# Define the mapping for the dense vector field
mapping = {
'properties': {
'embedding': {
'type': 'dense_vector',
dims': 768 # the number of dimensions of the dense vector
```

```
}
}
}
# Create an index with the defined mapping
es.indices.create(index='chapter-2', body={'mappings': mapping})

# Define a set of documents
docs = [
{
'title': 'Document 1',
'text': 'This is the first document.'
},
{
'title': 'Document 2',
'text': 'This is the second document.'
},
{
'title': 'Document 3',
'text': 'This is the third document.'
}
]

# Load the BERT tokenizer and model
tokenizer = AutoTokenizer.from_pretrained('bert-base-uncased')
model = AutoModel.from_pretrained('bert-base-uncased')

# Generate embeddings for the documents using BERT
for doc in docs:
text = doc['text']
inputs = tokenizer(text, return_tensors='pt', padding=True,
truncation=True)
with torch.no_grad():
output = model(**inputs).last_hidden_state.mean(dim=1).squeeze(0).
numpy()
doc['embedding'] = output.tolist()
# Index the documents in Elasticsearch
for doc in docs:  es.index(index='chapter-2', body=doc)
```

You can learn more about hidden units in the blog post at https://medium.com/computronium/hidden-units-in-neural-networks-b6a79b299a52, but essentially, each hidden unit in a neural network is associated with a set of weights and bias term that are learned during the training process. They determine how the hidden unit processes its input and produces its output.

The number of hidden units in a hidden layer is a hyperparameter of the network, and it can have a significant impact on a network's performance. A larger number of hidden units will benefit NLP use cases, since it allows the network to learn more complex representations of the input data. However, it makes the network more computationally expensive to train and evaluate.

The preceding example assumes you have a running Elasticsearch instance, as set up in the previous section. We used a BERT tokenizer and model to generate the embeddings for each document, which are finally indexed in Elasticsearch.

If you try to fetch the document, from **Kibana | Management | Dev Tools**, you should see something like this:

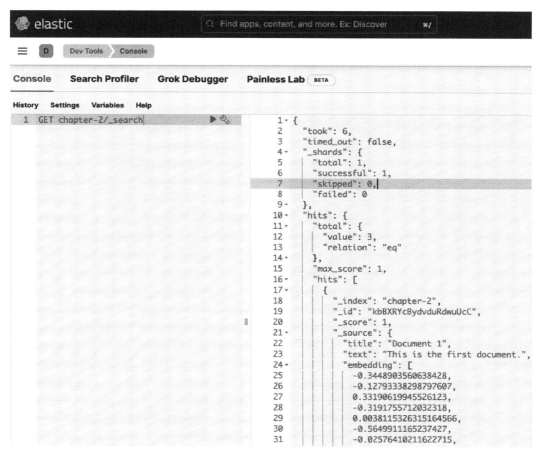

Figure 2.10: The embedding field showed in Kibana

You will see your documents with the `embedding` field containing the dense vectors.

There are some caveats if you don't customize the mapping slightly, which we will look at in the next section.

Brute-force kNN search

As said, there is a caveat with the previous example, and it concerns the fact that the vector field is not indexed by default, which means that you cannot use it with the kNN endpoint. You can use the vectors in the script score function, with a couple of similarity functions available out of the box to perform a brute-force or exact kNN search, as explained at this link: `https://www.elastic.co/guide/en/elasticsearch/reference/current/query-dsl-script-score-query.html#vector-functions`. The script scoring query is particularly useful when you want to avoid applying the scoring function on all documents searches, and only apply it on the filtered set of documents. The drawback is that the more filtered the document, the more expensive the script score can be, and it linearly increases.

Elasticsearch offers the following out-of-the-box similarity functions:

- `CosineSimilarity`: Calculates cosine similarity
- `dotProduct`: Calculates the dot product
- `l1norm`: Calculates the L1 distance
- `l2norm`: Calculates the L2 distance
- `doc[<field>].vectorValue`: Returns a vector's value as an array of floats
- `doc[<field>].magnitude`: Returns a vector's magnitude

Thankfully, at this stage of the chapter, you have a good understanding of what the preceding represents, and you also know that the recommended similarities for vectors are the first four options.

As a rule of thumb, if the number of documents after filtering is under 10,000 documents, then not indexing and using one of the similarity functions should give good performance.

The last two options refer to situations where you want to access vectors directly. While it gives an important level of control to users, the performance of the code will depend on how narrowed down the document set is and the quality of the script on multidimensional vectors.

kNN search

In this section, we'll explore how to activate kNN search for your indices and execute an illustrative example.

Mapping

Now, to be able to use kNN search, you need to modify the mapping so that the dense vectors are indexed, as follows:

```
{
  "mappings": {
    "properties": {
      "embedding": {
        "type": "dense_vector",
        "dims": 768,
        "index": true,
        "similarity": "dot_product",
      }
    }
  }
}
```

Note that you also need to set the similarity function. The three options for the similarity are `l2_norm`, `dot_product`, and `cosine`. We recommend, when possible, to use `dot_product` for vector search in production. Using the dot product avoids you having to calculate the vector magnitudes for every similarity computation (because the vectors are normalized in advance to all have a magnitude of 1). This means it can improve search and indexing speed by ~2-3x.

The difference with the brute-force kNN search based on the script scoring query is that, in this case, the HNSW graph is built and stored in memory. In fact, it is stored at the segment level, and this is why:

- Force merging is recommended at the index level to merge all the segments in an index into a single segment. It will not only optimize the search performance but also avoid HNSW being rebuilt at any segments. To merge all segments, the following API can be called:

  `POST /my-index/_forcemerge?max_num_segments=1`

- Updating a document, thus the dense vector, is not recommended at scale, since this would rebuild the HNSW again.

An example illustrating the use of kNN search

As a reminder, the kNN search API is used to find the *k* approximate nearest neighbors to a query vector. The query is also a vector of numbers that represent the text search query. The *k* nearest neighbors are the documents whose vectors are the most similar to the query vector.

The following example illustrates a fun way to use Elastic to build a jokes database. In this, the Python notebook builds a joke index, where the BERT model is used to represent jokes as vectors. It vectorizes a query string and then uses it in a kNN search to get similar jokes.

We start by importing the dependencies and defining the connection to our cluster:

```
!pip install transformers elasticsearch
import numpy as np
from transformers import AutoTokenizer, AutoModel
from elasticsearch import Elasticsearch
import torch

es = Elasticsearch(
['https://host:port'],
http_auth=('username', 'password'),
verify_certs=False
)

Then we set our index mapping as well as defining couple of documents
representing jokes:
mapping = {
'properties': {
'embedding': {
'type': 'dense_vector',
'dims': 768,
'index': 'true',
"similarity": "cosine"
}
}
}

es.indices.create(index='jokes-index', body={'mappings': mapping})


jokes = [
{
'text': 'Why do cats make terrible storytellers? Because they only
have one tail.',
'category': 'cat'
},
[.... other funny dad jokes ... ]
{
'text': 'Why did the frog call his insurance company? He had a jump in
his car!',
'category': 'puns'
}]
```

We will now load our BERT model, generate the embeddings, and index it in Elasticsearch:

```
# Load the BERT tokenizer and model
tokenizer = AutoTokenizer.from_pretrained('bert-base-uncased')
model = AutoModel.from_pretrained('bert-base-uncased')

# Generate embeddings for the jokes using BERT
for joke in jokes:
text = joke['text']
inputs = tokenizer(text, return_tensors='pt', padding=True,
truncation=True)
with torch.no_grad():
output = model(**inputs).last_hidden_state.mean(dim=1).squeeze(0).
numpy()
joke['embedding'] = output.tolist()

# Index the jokes in Elasticsearch
for joke in jokes:
es.index(index='jokes-index', body=joke)
```

Lastly, we define a query, convert it to a query vector, and run a vector search in Elasticsearch:

```
query = "What do you get when you cross a snowman and a shark?"
inputs = tokenizer(query, return_tensors='pt', padding=True,
truncation=True)
with torch.no_grad():
output = model(**inputs).last_hidden_state.mean(dim=1).squeeze(0).
numpy()
query_vector = output

# Define the Elasticsearch kNN search
search = {
"knn": {
"field": "embedding",
"query_vector": query_vector.tolist(),
"k": 3,
"num_candidates": 100
},
"fields": [ "text" ]
}
# Perform the kNN search and print the results
response = es.search(index='jokes-index', body=search)
for hit in response['hits']['hits']:
    print(f"Joke: {hit['_source']['text']}")
```

Here, we use the joke, "What do you get when you cross a snowman and a shark?" as the query.

The joke is not present in the dataset but has a similar semantic to returned jokes:

```
Joke: What did the cat say when he lost all his money? I am paw.
Joke: Why do cats make terrible storytellers? Because they only have
one tail.
Joke: Why don't cats play poker in the jungle? Too many cheetahs.
```

Also, note the structure of the kNN search query:

```
search = {
"knn": {
"field": "embedding",
"query_vector": query_vector.tolist(),
"k": 3,
"num_candidates": 100
},
"fields": [ "text" ]
}
```

The query requires the dense vector field (here, the field called `embedding`) as well as the vector representation of the text query, k, and `num_candidates`.

In kNN search, the API first finds a certain number of approximate nearest neighbor candidates on each shard; the number is `num_candidates`. Then, it calculates the similarity between these candidates and the query vector, selecting *k* most similar results from each shard. Finally, the results from each shard are merged to obtain the top *k* nearest neighbors in the entire dataset.

Summary

At this stage of the book, you should have a pretty good understanding of the fundamentals of vector search, including vector representation, how vectors are organized in an HNSW graph, and the method to calculate similarity between vectors. In addition, we have seen how to set up your Elastic Cloud environment as well as your Elasticsearch mapping to run Vector Search queries and leverage the *k*-nearest neighbors algorithm.

Now, you are equipped with the fundamental knowledge to explore all the subsequent chapters. We'll discover vector search domains of applications in various code examples and fields such as observability and security.

In the following chapter, we will go a step further – we'll not only learn how to host a model and generate vectors within Elasticsearch, as opposed to handling it externally, but also explore the intricacies of managing it at different scales and optimizing a deployment from a resource standpoint.

Part 2: Advanced Applications and Performance Optimization

Dive into the more complex aspects of vector search in Elastic, focusing on model management and performance tuning. These chapters are written for those who are ready to take their knowledge to the next level, offering insights into optimizing search functionalities and enhancing system performance. It's an in-depth look at the practical applications and fine-tuning required for efficient vector search deployment.

This part has the following chapters:

- *Chapter 3, Model Management and Vector Considerations in Elastic*
- *Chapter 4, Performance Tuning – Working with Data*

3

Model Management and Vector Considerations in Elastic

In this chapter, we will provide an overview of the Hugging Face ecosystem, Elasticsearch's Eland Python library, and practical strategies for using embedding models in Elasticsearch.

We will start by exploring the Hugging Face platform, discussing how to get started, selecting suitable models, and leveraging its vast collection of datasets. We will also delve into the features offered by Hugging Face's Spaces and how to use them effectively.

Then, we will introduce the Eland Python library, created by Elastic, and demonstrate its usage through a Jupyter Notebook example.

The topics that we will cover in this chapter are as follows:

- Eland Python library created by Elastic
- Index mappings
- **Machine Learning** (**ML**) nodes
- Integrating ML models into Elasticsearch
- Critical aspects of planning for cluster capacity
- Storage efficiency strategies that can help optimize the performance and resource utilization of your Elasticsearch cluster

Technical requirements

In order to implement the concepts covered in this chapter, you'll need the following:

- Elasticsearch 8.6 or later: `https://www.elastic.co/downloads/elasticsearch`

- Eland 8.6 or later: `https://eland.readthedocs.io/en/latest/index.html`

- Python 3.7 or later: `https://www.python.org/downloads/`

- pandas 1.3 or later: `https://pandas.pydata.org/docs/getting_started/install.html`

Hugging Face

As discussed briefly in the introduction, the primary goal of Hugging Face is to democratize access to state-of-the-art NLP technologies and facilitate their adoption across various industries and applications. By providing an extensive library of pre-trained models (over 120,000 at the time of this writing), user-friendly APIs, and a collaborative environment for model sharing and fine-tuning, Hugging Face empowers developers and researchers to create advanced language processing applications with ease.

Building upon that foundation, Hugging Face doesn't just stop at providing an extensive library; it also ensures streamlined access and effective application management. One of the standout features to this end is the Model Hub.

Model Hub

Hugging Face offers resources and services focused on the needs of both researchers and businesses. These include the Model Hub, which serves as a central repository for pre-trained models including inference APIs that allow easy access to these models.

Models can be searched for by name or task and easily filtered down by task type architecture, and more, to find the model for your use case. In *Figure 3.1*, you can see a list of models available when we search for the term `bert`:

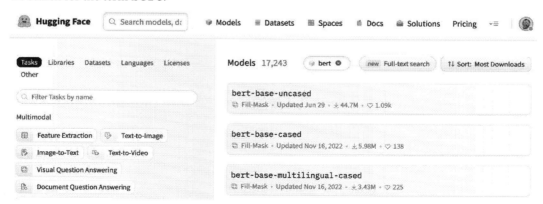

Figure 3.1: Hugging Face model's search results page

Selecting a model will provide you with information about the model. Across the top, you will see the task type, various architectures it is available in, libraries used, language, license, and more. In *Figure 3.2*, we see information about the **bert-base-uncased** model:

Figure 3.2: Hugging Face Model Card summary information

Most models, especially the more popular ones, have a **Model Card**. A Model Card contains information provided by the developer, such as how the model was trained, a detailed description, model variations, related models, intended uses and limitations, code examples for running, known bias, and information about how it was trained. In *Figure 3.3*, we see information about how the BERT model was trained:

Figure 3.3: Model training and description information

In *Figure 3.4*, we can see how many downloads were made in the last month, and often the most useful, a live interface to the Hosted Inference API. A Hosted Inference API allows programmatic access to a model running on Hugging Face shared infrastructure that will accept input, process it through a model, and return the output. This API UI will allow you to test the model by providing input and seeing the output.

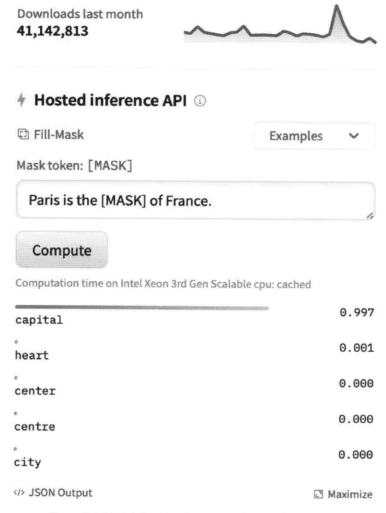

Figure 3.4: Model download counts and test inference API

Having discussed the relevance of the Model Hub and its various features, it's equally imperative to shed light on the underlying data that powers these models. Enter **Hugging Face Datasets**, a cornerstone in the landscape of NLP and ML data utilities.

Datasets

Hugging Face Datasets is a library designed to simplify the process of downloading, pre-processing, and utilizing diverse datasets for various NLP and ML tasks. This library offers access to a large collection of datasets, covering a wide range of topics and languages, and caters to a multitude of use cases, such as sentiment analysis, translation, and summarization. The datasets are sourced from research papers, web scraping, or user contributions, and they are made available to the community in a standardized format. One of the key features of Hugging Face Datasets is its direct integration with the **Transformers** library, enabling users to easily combine these datasets with NLP models for training, evaluation, and deployment.

Using Hugging Face Datasets is straightforward.

To get started, you need to install the library using `pip install datasets`. Once the library is installed, you can load a dataset by simply importing the library and using the `load_dataset()` function. For example, if you want to load the IMDb movie reviews dataset for sentiment analysis, you can use the following code:

```
from datasets import load_dataset
imdb_dataset = load_dataset("imdb")
```

Hugging Face Datasets also offers useful features for dataset pre-processing and manipulation, including filtering, mapping, and shuffling. These functions enable users to easily prepare the data for use with their models. In this example, we will tokenize the IMDb dataset using a pre-trained tokenizer from the Transformers library:

```
from datasets import load_dataset
from transformers import AutoTokenizer

# Load a small portion of the IMDB dataset (100 samples)
imdb_dataset = load_dataset("imdb", split="train[:100]")

# Initialize the tokenizer
tokenizer = AutoTokenizer.from_pretrained("bert-base-uncased")

# Tokenize the IMDB dataset with truncation and padding
tokenized_imdb_dataset = imdb_dataset.map(
lambda x: tokenizer(x["text"], truncation=True, padding="max_length")
)

print(tokenized_imdb_dataset)
# This prints out:
Dataset({
    features: ['text', 'label', 'input_ids', 'token_type_ids',
'attention_mask'],
```

```
    num_rows: 100
})


# Get the first row of tokens
first_row_tokens = tokenized_imdb_dataset[0]["input_ids"]

# Print the first 10 tokens and their corresponding words
for token in first_row_tokens[:10]:
print(f"Token: {token}, Word: {tokenizer.decode([token])}")
```

This prints out the following:

```
Token: 101,Word: [CLS]
Token: 1045, Word: i
Token: 12524, Word: rented
Token: 1045, Word: i
Token: 2572, Word: am
Token: 8025, Word: curious
Token: 1011, Word: -
Token: 3756, Word: yellow
Token: 2013, Word: from
Token: 2026, Word: my
```

In the output, we can see that when we run `imdb_dataset['text'][0]`, we get the first 10 tokens and the corresponding words from the first row of IMDb input.

Spaces

Hugging Face Spaces is a platform designed to facilitate the deployment, sharing, and collaboration of ML models, particularly those focused on NLP. With Spaces, users can easily deploy their models as interactive web applications, powered by *Gradio* or *Streamlit*, without the need for additional infrastructure or complex configurations. Spaces allows users to showcase their work, gather feedback, and collaborate with others in the community, making it an invaluable tool for both experienced practitioners and beginners in the field of ML and NLP.

One of the key features of Hugging Face Spaces is its seamless integration with the Hugging Face ecosystem, including the Transformers library and the Hugging Face Hub. This integration allows users to quickly deploy their pre-trained or fine-tuned models as interactive applications, enabling others to test the models and gain insights into their capabilities. To get started with Spaces, users need to create an account on the Hugging Face website and follow the guidelines for deploying a new Space. The process typically involves writing a Python script that leverages the *Gradio* or *Streamlit* framework, importing the desired model from the Hugging Face Hub, and defining the user interface components for interaction with the model.

Let's look at the code that will allow you to set up a simple *Gradio* interface:

```python
import gradio as gr
from transformers import pipeline
sentiment_pipeline = pipeline("sentiment-analysis")

def sentiment_analysis(text):
    result = sentiment_pipeline(text)
    return result[0]["label"]

iface = gr.Interface(fn=sentiment_analysis, inputs="text",
outputs="text")
iface.launch()
```

In this example, a sentiment analysis pipeline is created using the Hugging Face Transformers library, and a *Gradio* interface is defined to accept text input and display the sentiment label as output. Once the code is uploaded to a Hugging Face Space, users can interact with the application through a web browser, testing the sentiment analysis model with their own text inputs. Spaces offers a simple yet powerful way to showcase ML models and foster collaboration within the community.

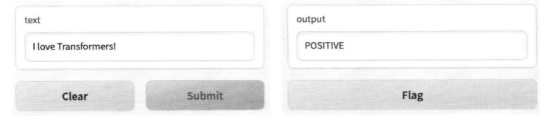

Figure 3.5: Simple example of testing a sentiment analysis model

While Hugging Face Spaces provides an exceptional platform for NLP applications, Hugging Face is not the only resource we have to work with. Let's diversify our toolkit by shifting our focus to Eland and its role in bridging the gap between Elasticsearch and traditional data processing frameworks such as pandas.

Eland

Eland is a Python library developed by Elastic that allows users to interface with Elasticsearch seamlessly for data manipulation and analysis. The library is built on top of the official Elasticsearch Python client and extends the **pandas API** to Elasticsearch. This enables users to interact with Elasticsearch data using familiar pandas-like syntax and conventions, making it easier to integrate Elasticsearch with existing data analysis workflows and tools.

Eland is particularly useful for handling large datasets that cannot fit in memory and require distributed processing. Elasticsearch can scale horizontally by distributing data across multiple nodes in a cluster. This allows the user to efficiently work with far larger datasets than what would be possible on a laptop. Let's look at some features of Eland:

- One key use case for Eland is querying data stored in Elasticsearch. Instead of writing raw Elasticsearch queries, users can write Python code that resembles pandas syntax to filter, sort, and aggregate data. For example, you can fetch data from an Elasticsearch index as follows:

```
import eland as ed

df = ed.DataFrame("http://localhost:9200", "my_index")
filtered_df = df[df['some_field'] > 100]
```

- In addition to data querying and transformation, Eland supports aggregations, enabling users to generate summary statistics or compute complex aggregations on Elasticsearch data. This can be useful for understanding the distribution and characteristics of large datasets. Here's an example of how to compute the average value of a specific field:

```
average_value = df['some_field'].mean()
```

- Eland can also be used for data visualization, as it integrates seamlessly with popular Python visualization libraries such as Matplotlib and Seaborn. Once you have fetched and manipulated data using Eland, you can easily convert the result to a pandas DataFrame and create visualizations. Here's an example:

```
import seaborn as sns
import pandas as pd

filtered_df = df[df['some_field'] > 100]
pandas_df = filtered_df.to_pandas()
sns.boxplot(x='category', y='value', data=pandas_df)
```

Recently, Eland has been extended to import NLP transformers models into Elasticsearch. Elasticsearch currently supports a select set of architecture that has been trained in PyTorch and conforms to the standard BERT model interface. This allows Elasticsearch to natively run NLP tasks such as **named entity recognition**, **zero-shot classification**, **question-answering**, and more. The current list of supported tasks can be viewed in the docs: https://www.elastic.co/guide/en/machine-learning/current/ml-nlp-model-ref.html.

Most relevant to this book is the native support for text embedding models. Eland is used to either load a locally stored model, or more commonly, load a model directly from Hugging Face into Elasticsearch. The model is downloaded and then chunked up so it can be loaded into Elasticsearch.

Now we will walk through a Jupyter notebook in which we will configure an Elasticsearch connection, load a model from Hugging Face, deploy (start) the model, and generate a test vector.

The full code can be viewed in the book's Jupyter Notebook in the chapter 3 folder in the book's GitHub repository: https://github.com/PacktPublishing/Vector-Search-for-Practitioners-with-Elastic/tree/main/chapter3.

With the foundational understanding of how Eland facilitates the integration of Hugging Face models with Elasticsearch, let's delve deeper into the practical aspects of using the code. Next, we will navigate the steps to efficiently load a Sentence Transformer from Hugging Face directly into Elasticsearch, elucidating the process for those looking to harness the combined power of these platforms.

Loading a Sentence Transformer from Hugging Face into Elasticsearch

This code will show you how to load a supported embedding model from Hugging Face into an Elasticsearch cluster in Elastic Cloud: https://cloud.elastic.co/.

Here, we will install and import the required Python libraries:

- eland
- elasticsearch
- transformers
- sentence_transformers
- torch==1.11

Elastic uses the Eland library to download models from the Hugging Face Hub and load them into Elasticsearch:

```
pip -q install eland elasticsearch transformers sentence_transformers
torch==1.13
from pathlib import Path
from eland.ml.pytorch import PyTorchModel
from eland.ml.pytorch.transformers import TransformerModel
from elasticsearch import Elasticsearch
from elasticsearch.client import MlClient
```

Configuring Elasticsearch authentication

The recommended authentication approach uses the Elastic Cloud ID (https://www.elastic.co/guide/en/cloud/current/ec-cloud-id.html) and a cluster-level API key (https://www.elastic.co/guide/en/kibana/current/api-keys.html).

You can use any method you wish to set the required credentials. We are using getpass in this example to prompt for credentials to avoid storing them in GitHub:

```
import getpass
es_cloud_id = getpass.getpass('Enter Elastic Cloud ID:  ') es_api_id
= getpass.getpass('Enter cluster API key ID:  ') es_api_key = getpass.
getpass('Enter cluster API key:  ')
# Connect to Elastic Cloud
es = Elasticsearch(cloud_id=es_cloud_id, api_key=(es_api_id, es_api_
key))
es.info() # should return cluster info
```

Loading a model from the Hugging Face Hub

The Elastic Stack ML features support transformer models that conform to the standard BERT model interface and use the WordPiece tokenization algorithm.

For an in-depth explanation of WordPiece tokenization, check out this section of the Hugging Face NLP course: https://huggingface.co/learn/nlp-course/chapter6/6?fw=pt.

Download an embedding model from Hugging Face using the copy link as shown in *Figure 3.6*.

For this example, we will be using the sentence-transformers/msmarco-MiniLM-L-12-v3 model: https://huggingface.co/sentence-transformers/msmarco-MiniLM-L-12-v3.

Downloading the model

Here, we specify the model ID from Hugging Face. The easiest way to get this ID is by clicking the icon to copy the model name, which is next to the name on the model page.

Figure 3.6: Copy location for model_id

When calling TransformerModel, you specify the Hugging Face model's ID and the task type. You can try specifying auto and Eland will attempt to determine the correct type from the information in the model configuration. This is not always possible, so a list of specific task_type can be set:

```
hf_model_id='sentence-transformers/msmarco-MiniLM-L-12-v3'
tm = TransformerModel( model_id=hf_model_id, task_type="text_
embedding")
```

Next, we set and confirm the model ID. To make the name compatible with Elasticsearch, the / is replaced with ___ (double underscore):

```
es_model_id = tm.elasticsearch_model_id()
```

Export the model in a TorchScrpt representation, which Elasticsearch uses:

```
tmp_path = "models"
Path(tmp_path).mkdir(parents=True, exist_ok=True)
model_path, config, vocab_path = tm.save(tmp_path)
```

Loading the model into Elasticsearch

Here, the model will be serialized and loaded into Elasticsearch so it can then be started on an ML node:

```
ptm = PyTorchModel(es, es_model_id)
ptm.import_model(model_path=model_path, config_path=None, vocab_
path=vocab_path, config=config)
```

Starting the model

This step will give us information about the model, such as the name and status, as the output:

```
# List the in Elasticsearch
m = MlClient.get_trained_models(es, model_id=es_model_id)
```

Deploying the model

The following code will load the model on the ML nodes and start the process(es) of making it available for the NLP task:

```
s = MlClient.start_trained_model_deployment(es, model_id=es_model_id)
```

Next, we will verify that the model starts without an issue:

```
stats = MlClient.get_trained_models_stats(es, model_id=es_model_id)
stats.body['trained_model_stats'][0]['deployment_stats']['nodes'][0]
['routing_state']
```

You should see the following output, letting you know the model has been deployed to the ML nodes:

```
{'routing_state': 'started'}
```

Generating a vector for a query

Before we can run a kNN query, we need to convert our query string to a vector.

Next, we will create an example query sentence to verify that everything has been set up correctly:

```
docs = [
    {
        "text_field": "Last week I upgraded my iOS version and ever
since then my phone has been overheating whenever I use your app."
    }
]
```

We call the _infer endpoint, which supplies the model_id and the document/s we want to vectorize:

```
z = MlClient.infer_trained_model(es, model_id=es_model_id, docs=docs,
)
```

The vector for the first doc can be accessed in the response dictionary, as shown here:

```
doc_0_vector = z['inference_results'][0]['predicted_value']
doc_0_vector
```

With the embedding model loaded and successfully tested, we can now use it in a production setting.

Generating vectors in Elasticsearch

Vectors can be generated during ingest before a document is indexed (written) into Elasticsearch using an ingest pipeline. Each processor in the ingest pipeline performs a different task, such as enriching, modifying, or removing data. The key processor in that pipeline is the inference processor, which passes the text to an embedding model, receives the vector representation, and then adds the vector to the original document payload before moving it along to be stored in an index. This ensures that the document's vector representation is available for indexing and searching immediately after it is ingested.

Coming up is an example of an Elasticsearch ingest pipeline configuration that uses the inference processor with the **sentence-transformers/msmarco-MiniLM-L-12-v3** model we loaded earlier. The pipeline takes a field named summary from the input document, processes it using the embedding model to generate an embedding, and stores the resulting vector in a field named vector.

Here, we are using HTTP calls rather than Python code to demonstrate an alternate approach to Python. Note that the model is assumed to already be loaded in the cluster, since we did that in an earlier example:

```
PUT _ingest/pipeline/embedding_book_pipeline
{
    "description": "Ingest pipeline using bert-base-uncased model",
```

```
    "processors": [
      {
        "inference": {
            "target_field": "vector",
            "model_id": "sentence-transformers__msmarco-minilm-1-12-v3",
            "field_map": {
              "summary": "text_field"
            }
        }
      }
    ]
}
```

To use this ingest pipeline when indexing a document, include the `pipeline` parameter in the index request:

```
PUT my_index/_doc/1?pipeline=embedding_book_pipeline
{
  "summary": "This is an example text for the embedding model."
}
```

This request will index a document with the provided text field and an additional vector field containing the embedding generated by the bert-base-uncased model.

The `_infer` endpoint can also be called directly to generate vectors either at query time (see the next section) or for any other ad hoc reason:

```
POST _ml/trained_models/sentence-transformers__msmarco-minilm-1-
12-v3/_infer
{
    "docs": [
{"text_field": "How do I load an NLP model from Hugging Face"}
]
}
```

This will return a 200 response code and a vector representation of the submitted text:

```
{
  "inference_results": [
    {
      "predicted_value": [
        0.012806695885956287,
        -0.04550656303037633896,
        0.014663844369351864,
  ...
        0.002125605707988143,
```

```
            0.06371472030878067
        ]
      }
    ]
}
```

At search time, the `_infer` endpoint can be called to generate a vector from input text, which can then be used as part of a vector search query. Here, we will take the vector we generated previously and use it as part of a kNN query:

```
GET search-elastic-docs-vectorized/_search
{
  "knn": {
    "field": "body_content-vector",
    "k": 1,
    "num_candidates": 20,
    "query_vector": [
        0.012806695885956287,
        -0.045506563037633896,
        0.014663844369351864,
  ...
        0.002125605707988143,
        0.06371472030878067
      ]
  },
  "fields": [ "body_content", "headings" ],
  "_source": false
}
```

Alternatively, an embedding model can be specified as part of the _knn query (after Elasticsearch 8.7), and Elasticsearch will handle generating the query vector before running the rest of the _knn query. This allows more streamlined integration of vector search capabilities and simplifies the kNN search process:

```
GET search-elastic-docs-vectorized/_search
{
  "knn": {
    "field": "dense-vector-field",
    "k": 10,
    "num_candidates": 100,
    "query_vector_builder": {
      "text_embedding": {
        "model_id": "my-text-embedding-model",
```

```
        "model_text": "The opposite of blue"
      }
    }
  }
}
```

Let's see how we can plan for cluster capacity and resources in a production environment.

Planning for cluster capacity and resources

Planning for sufficient cluster capacity and resources is crucial for any production environment, especially when implementing a vector search use case of considerable size. To ensure optimal performance and efficiency, careful consideration, planning, and testing must be carried out.

In the following chapter, we will delve into load testing, which is an essential part of fine-tuning and optimizing your Elasticsearch deployment. But before that, we will explore what it takes to run embedding models on ML nodes in Elasticsearch, outlining the essential factors to consider in order to strike the right balance between performance and resource utilization. In this section, we will discuss the critical aspects of CPU, RAM, and disk requirements, setting the stage for a comprehensive understanding of resource management in Elasticsearch.

CPU and memory requirements

The CPU requirements for vector search in Elasticsearch are not drastically different from those of traditional search. The primary distinction lies in how vector data is accessed during **approximate kNN** (which we'll refer to as **kNN** for simplicity here) queries.

In traditional search and brute-force/exact match vector search, as more documents are added, the disk space is scaled out, and the CPU is scaled up to accommodate increased throughput.

The same is true in kNN search with Elasticsearch; however, for the fastest response times, we want enough off-heap RAM available to load all the vector embeddings into memory. When there isn't enough RAM available outside of the Elasticsearch JVM to fit the embeddings, Elasticsearch will have to read from disk, leading to a slower response time when this is done frequently. This shift in data access method can lead to improved performance because it has been observed that hot threads are more likely to occur when vectors have to be read from the disk rather than directly from memory. By accessing the data directly from off-heap RAM, vector search reduces the impact of these hot threads and provides a more efficient querying process.

> **Note**
>
> hot_threads is a diagnostic API that provides insights into the busiest internal tasks currently running in an Elasticsearch node. It helps identify performance bottlenecks by highlighting threads that are consuming unusually high CPU resources.

With page-cache memory requirements being particularly important to kNN search, users need to be mindful of how many vectors fit in a node's available page-cache RAM. Assuming the default configurations for **Hierarchical Navigable Small World** (**HNSW**) are used, a loose calculation for the number of bytes required is as follows:

```
num_vectors * 4 * (num_dimensions + 12) = total RAM in bytes
```

As an example, if you are using a model that outputs 512-dimensional vectors and you expect to load 20 million vectors into Elasticsearch, the formula would look like this:

```
20,000,000 * 4 * (512 + 12) = 41,920,000,000 bytes
41,920,000,000 / 1024 ~= 39 GB RAM
```

Twenty million embedding fields translates to a loose estimate of requiring approximately 39 GB of off-heap RAM for kNN search to be most performant. If you consider a full-sized node in Elasticsearch to be 64 GB—half going to the Elasticsearch JVM, and several GB going to the OS and any other processes—you are left with a starting estimate of 2 data nodes to handle those vectors. Also, keep in mind that is without considering replicas.

This is a starting estimate and a good place for when you start your testing. It is not intended to be an exact RAM requirement. Testing, covered later in the chapter, will give you the best numbers before moving to production.

Having set the stage with the requirements and implications of RAM usage, we pivot our attention to another critical resource in the ecosystem: storage.

Disk requirements

As we've seen, one of the primary considerations for performant kNN search is ensuring there is adequate off-heap RAM available to store vectors. However, it is important to note that those vectors are still generated and stored on disk. As such, users have to ensure there is adequate storage available. However, due to the size of disks versus the size of RAM, disk capacity is generally not the limiting factor when planning cluster capacity.

The formula to estimate the required RAM mentioned in the previous section is the same calculation for disk capacity for vector data, but you will also have to take into consideration any other fields you are storing along with the vectors, such as the text of the vectors, other text fields, and metadata.

A rough starting estimate for disk capacity is as follows:

```
size of a single document * number of documents * number of replicas *
1.2
```

Here, 1.2 is the net multiplier between JSON expansion and disk compression. Please note that this is a very rough estimate.

However, the only true way to get an idea of how your data will behave in Elasticsearch is to load a sample dataset. You can easily use a free trial of Elastic Cloud to spin up a small cluster and load a small representative dataset. Starting a trial is quick and only requires an email address at `https://cloud.elastic.co/registration`.

You will have access to a small, fully functional Elasticsearch cluster including an ML node and all Enterprise features. The *Getting Started* guides at `https://www.elastic.co/getting-started` can help you get up and running quickly.

Once you have loaded your data, you'll be able to see the exact size your data will expand out to, which is the only true way to plan for your production requirements. Even past the free trial, you can grow your cluster slowly if needed with easy month-to-month payments.

You can use the disk usage API covered in the next section to see disk usage, and we cover cluster tuning, load testing, and full scaling testing in the next chapter.

Now that we've discussed the importance of understanding your data size and scaling implications, it's paramount to have tools that provide precise insights into the real-world utilization of these resources. One such crucial tool in the Elasticsearch suite is the analyze disk usage API. Let's explore its functionality and how it aids in understanding disk space consumption.

Analyze Index Disk Usage API

Once vectors (and any other data) have been loaded into Elasticsearch, you can use the **analyze index disk usage API** to calculate how much disk space is being taken up. For more information on the analyze disk usage API, visit the documentation page at `https://www.elastic.co/guide/en/elasticsearch/reference/current/indices-disk-usage.html`.

The `search-elastic-docs` index has multiple vector fields that are relatively small in data size. One of those is `title-vector`:

```
POST /search-elastic-docs/_disk_usage?run_expensive_tasks=true&pretty
```

This gives the following response (the full response of the API call is very long, so we are only showing the truncated output containing relevant parts here):

```
{
  "_shards": {
    "total": 2,
    "successful": 2,
    "failed": 0
  },
  "search-elastic-docs": {
    "store_size": "989.5mb",
    "store_size_in_bytes": 1037592858,
```

```
    "all_fields": {
      "total": "987.6mb",
      "total_in_bytes": 1035596641,
      "inverted_index": {
        "total": "69.8mb",
        "total_in_bytes": 73269048
      },
...
      "knn_vectors": "83.4mb",
      "knn_vectors_in_bytes": 87462952
    },
    "fields": {
...
      "title-vector": {
        "total": "40mb",
        "total_in_bytes": 42046916,
        "inverted_index": {
          "total": "0b",
          "total_in_bytes": 0
        },
...
        "knn_vectors": "40mb",
        "knn_vectors_in_bytes": 42046916
      },
...
```

We can see that the vectors are taking up 83.4 MB. With disk usage analyzed, we can turn our attention to ML node capacity planning.

ML node capacity

For embedding models run on ML nodes in Elasticsearch, you will need to plan to ensure your nodes have enough capacity to run the model at inference time. Elastic Cloud allows the auto-scaling of ML nodes based on CPU requirements, which allows them to scale up and out when more compute is required and scale down when those requirements are reduced.

We cover tuning ML nodes for inference in the next chapter in more detail, but minimally, you will need an ML node with enough RAM to load at least one instance of the embedding model. As your performance requirements increase, you can increase the number of allocations of the individual model as well as the number of threads allocated per allocation.

To check the size of a model and the amount of memory (RAM) required to load the model, you can run the **get trained models statistics API** (for more information on this API, visit the documentation page at https://www.elastic.co/guide/en/elasticsearch/reference/current/get-trained-models-stats.html#get-trained-models-stats):

```
GET _ml/trained_models/dslim__bert-base-ner-uncased/_stats?human
```

This will return various stats, including model size and memory requirements:

```
{

        "model_id": "dslim__bert-base-ner-uncased",
        "model_size_stats": {
          "model_size": "415.4mb",
          "model_size_bytes": 435663717,
          "required_native_memory": "1gb",
          "required_native_memory_bytes": 1122985674
        },
```

When a model is running, you can also get stats about it in the Kibana UI by going to **Machine Learning** > **Model Management** > **Trained Models** and expanding the model ID.

When planning ML node capacity, two distinct situations need to be considered:

- **At indexing time**: Generally, there is an initial large bulk load of documents into an Elasticsearch index, which requires vector generation. This will put a large demand on your ML nodes to run inference as quickly as possible. This is where the ability to easily scale ML nodes and increase the number of model allocations dynamically is very useful. You can scale out the model allocations while your initial bulk load is running, and then reduce the allocations when that load is complete.

- **Around search time inference**: When a search query is sent by a user, you will need to use the same embedding model to generate a query vector that you used to generate the document vector. Keeping up with your average query load will allow you to plan your normal operating size. Should you have a planned spike in query load approaching, for example, a busy shopping weekend in e-commerce, you can proactively increase the number of model allocations and, in turn, scale the ML nodes.

The only true way to test both of these conditions is with load testing and performance tuning on your actual data, which we cover in more depth in the next chapter.

Storage efficiency strategies

As your production dataset for vector search grows in size, so do the resources required to store those vectors and search through them in a timely fashion. In this section, we discuss several strategies users can take to reduce those resources. Each strategy has its trade-offs and should be carefully considered and thoroughly tested before being put into production.

Reducing dimensionality

Reducing dimensionality refers to the process of transforming high-dimensional data into a lower-dimensional representation. This process is often employed to mitigate the challenges that arise when working with high-dimensional data, such as the **curse of dimensionality** (https://en.wikipedia.org/wiki/Curse_of_dimensionality). Dimensionality reduction techniques, such as **Principal Component Analysis** (**PCA**) and **t-Distributed Stochastic Neighbor Embedding** (**t-SNE**), can help improve the efficiency and effectiveness of kNN vector search. However, there are advantages and disadvantages associated with reducing dimensionality.

One significant advantage of dimensionality reduction is the reduction in storage, memory, and computational requirements. High-dimensional vector data can consume large amounts of RAM and CPU resources, making it challenging to work with in Elasticsearch. By transforming the data into a lower-dimensional representation, the amount of off-heap RAM and computation needed is reduced, potentially improving the efficiency of kNN vector search algorithms and enabling their application in resource-constrained environments.

Another advantage of reducing dimensionality is that it can help mitigate the curse of dimensionality, a phenomenon that arises when the number of dimensions increases and the data points become increasingly sparse. This sparsity can lead to poor performance of distance-based algorithms as the distances between data points in high-dimensional spaces become less meaningful. Reducing dimensionality can help alleviate this issue by effectively capturing the most relevant information in a lower-dimensional space, making distance-based search algorithms more effective.

However, there are some disadvantages to reducing dimensionality. One of the primary drawbacks is the potential loss of information. Dimensionality reduction techniques often involve some level of approximation or compression, which can lead to the loss of subtle relationships or nuances in the data. This loss of information can impact the accuracy and effectiveness of kNN vector search, as the reduced-dimensional representations may not fully capture the relationships between data points in the original high-dimensional space.

Another disadvantage is the added complexity and computational overhead associated with the dimensionality reduction process. Applying dimensionality reduction techniques typically requires additional computation and resources, which may offset some of the benefits gained from reducing the dimensionality of the data. Furthermore, selecting the appropriate dimensionality reduction technique and tuning its parameters can be challenging, as the optimal choice often depends on the specific characteristics of the data and the problem domain.

Here is an example using the Iris dataset, which has four dimensions, and reducing its dimensionality to two using PCA:

```python
import numpy as np
import matplotlib.pyplot as plt
from sklearn import datasets
from sklearn.decomposition import PCA

# Load the Iris dataset
iris = datasets.load_iris()
X = iris.data
y = iris.target

# Apply PCA for dimensionality reduction
pca = PCA(n_components=2)
X_reduced = pca.fit_transform(X)

# Visualize the original data
plt.scatter(X[:, 0], X[:, 1], c=y, cmap=plt.cm.Set1, edgecolor='k')
plt.xlabel('Sepal length')
plt.ylabel('Sepal width')
plt.title('Original Iris dataset')
plt.show()

# Visualize the reduced data
plt.scatter(X_reduced[:, 0], X_reduced[:, 1], c=y, cmap=plt.cm.Set1,
edgecolor='k')
plt.xlabel('First Principal Component')
plt.ylabel('Second Principal Component')
plt.title('Iris dataset after PCA')
plt.show()
```

The scatter plots in *Figure 3.7* show the distribution of the original data and the reduced data. Reducing the dimensionality results in some loss of information, but it can also make the data more manageable and improve the performance of distance-based algorithms, such as kNN search.

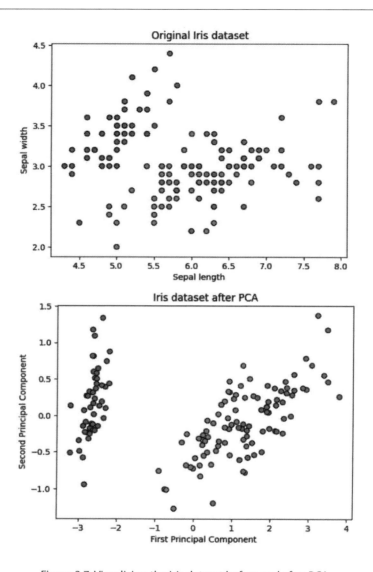

Figure 3.7: Visualizing the Iris dataset before and after PCA

Alternatively, some pre-trained models are released with different dimension sizes. If you are starting out with a pre-trained model that has these options, testing one of the smaller dimensional options would be worth doing before attempting dimensional reduction yourself.

Quantization

Quantization is a technique that's used in vector search to reduce the size and complexity of high-dimensional data while maintaining the ability to perform meaningful search operations. The process of quantization involves converting continuous vector values, often represented as floating-point numbers, into a smaller and more compact representation, such as integers. This transformation reduces the storage and computation requirements associated with high-dimensional data, enabling more efficient search and retrieval operations.

Moving from floating-point representations to 8-bit vectors can have a significant impact on the size and storage requirements of the data. Floating-point numbers typically require 32 or 64 bits to represent a single value, whereas an 8-byte vector uses only 8 bits per value. This reduction in size can lead to substantial savings in storage and memory requirements, enabling the efficient handling of large-scale vector search applications. However, this compression can come at the cost of reduced precision and accuracy, as the quantization process involves approximating the original floating-point values with a smaller number of discrete levels. This loss of precision may affect the relevancy of search results because the distances between quantized vectors may not perfectly reflect the relationships between data points in the original high-dimensional space.

To demonstrate the quantization process, let's use the Public Digits dataset available in the scikit-learn library, which is a smaller version of the MNIST dataset containing 8x8 pixel images of handwritten digits. This dataset is small enough to run on a laptop without requiring too much memory or computational power. We will use the PCA method for dimensionality reduction and then apply quantization to the reduced vectors:

```python
import numpy as np
from sklearn import datasets
from sklearn.decomposition import PCA
from sklearn.preprocessing import MinMaxScaler, QuantileTransformer

# Load the digits dataset
digits = datasets.load_digits()
X = digits.data

# Print the first example from the original dataset
print("Original dataset (first example):\n", X[0])

# Apply PCA for dimensionality reduction
pca = PCA(n_components=10)
X_reduced = pca.fit_transform(X)

# Print the first example after PCA
print("\nReduced dataset after PCA (first example):\n", X_reduced[0])

# Normalize the reduced vectors to the range [0, 255]
```

```
scaler = MinMaxScaler((0, 255))
X_scaled = scaler.fit_transform(X_reduced)

# Print the first example after normalization
print("\nScaled dataset after normalization (first example):\n", X_
scaled[0])

# Quantize the scaled vectors to 8-byte integers
X_quantized = np.round(X_scaled).astype(np.uint8)

# Print the first example after quantization
print("\nQuantized dataset (first example):\n", X_quantized[0])
```

This will output the following:

```
Original dataset (first example): [ 0. 0. 5. 13. 9. 1. 0. 0. 0. 0. 13.
15. 10. 15. 5. 0. 0. 3. 15. 2. 0. 11. 8. 0. 0. 4. 12. 0. 0. 8. 8. 0.
0. 5. 8. 0. 0. 9. 8. 0. 0. 4. 11. 0. 1. 12. 7. 0. 0. 2. 14. 5. 10. 12.
0. 0. 0. 0. 6. 13. 10. 0. 0. 0.]
Reduced dataset after PCA (first example): [-1.25943119 21.27487713
-9.4630716 13.01409073 -7.12874004 -7.44073278 3.25357601 2.55756705
-0.58760376 3.63146582]
Scaled dataset after normalization (first example): [121.31621096
215.95604417 81.58062648 168.0966397 77.88288852 73.75078201
132.99089292 135.63851202 121.03524697 151.29258751]
Quantized dataset (first example): [121 216 82 168 78 74 133 136 121
151]
```

As stated earlier, while this process can lead to significant storage and performance improvements, it may also result in reduced precision and search relevancy. When considering quantization, users should test the relevancy of search results before and after quantization to see whether the reduction is acceptable before moving into production.

Reducing dimensionality and quantization are two techniques used to optimize embedding models and vector representations, but they serve different purposes and address different aspects of the data. Reducing dimensionality targets the number of dimensions in the vector representation, while quantization focuses on reducing the precision of each element in the vector. Both techniques can improve efficiency and reduce memory requirements, but they may also introduce some loss of information or precision, which could affect the search results' accuracy and quality.

Having discussed the nuances of optimizing vector representations, it's essential to note that the efficiency of a system isn't just about the data itself but also about how it's stored and retrieved. With Elasticsearch and vector search, the _source field plays a pivotal role, especially when dealing with high-dimensional data. Let's discuss the implications of dense_vector within the _source field and its potential effects on search performance.

Excluding dense_vector from _source

Elasticsearch stores the original JSON document passed at index time in the _source field. By default, each match in the search results contains the full document. However, when the documents contain high-dimensional dense_vector fields, the _source field can become quite large, leading to substantial overhead in loading the data. As a result, the speed of kNN search may be significantly reduced due to the additional time required to process these larger _source fields.

To mitigate this issue, you can disable storing dense_vector fields in the _source by using the excludes mapping parameter. This approach prevents loading and returning large vectors during search operations, reducing both the processing overhead and the index size. Despite being omitted from the _source, the vectors can still be used in kNN search because the search process relies on separate data structures to perform the search efficiently.

Before applying the excludes parameter, it is important to understand the potential downsides of omitting fields from the _source. Doing so can limit the ability to documents or perform certain update operations that require access to the original field values.

An example of this setting in the mapping is as follows:

```
PUT my_index
{
  "mappings": {
    "_source": {
      "excludes": [
        "vector_field"
      ]
    },
    "properties": {
      "vector_field": {
        "type": "dense_vector",
        "dims": 384,
        "index" : True,
        "similarity" : "dot_product"
      },
      "text_field": {
        "type": "text"
      }
    }
  }
}
```

Unless you plan on re-indexing the field at some point, users should definitely consider setting this for any index with `dense_vector` fields as it will save space and increase kNN search speed.

Excluding `dense_vector` fields from the `_source` in Elasticsearch can lead to efficient kNN search speeds and reduced index size. However, users should weigh the benefits against potential re-indexing needs, ensuring an optimized and effective storage approach for their specific use case.

Summary

In this chapter, we delved into the intricacies of the Hugging Face ecosystem and the capabilities of Elasticsearch's Eland Python library, offering practical examples for using embedding models within Elasticsearch. We explored the Hugging Face platform, highlighting its datasets, model selection, and the potential of its Spaces. Furthermore, we provided a hands-on approach to the Eland library, illustrating its functionalities and addressing pivotal considerations such as mappings, ML nodes, and model integration. We also touched upon the nuances of cluster capacity planning, emphasizing RAM, disk size, and CPU considerations. Finally, we underscored several storage efficiency tactics, focusing on dimensionality reduction, quantization, and mapping settings to ensure optimal performance and resource conservation for your Elasticsearch cluster.

In the next chapter, we will dive into the operational phase of working with data and learn how to tune performance for interference and querying.

4

Performance Tuning – Working with Data

In the previous chapter, we covered how to integrate Elasticsearch with **machine learning (ML)** models. In this chapter, we'll focus on optimizing vector search performance in Elasticsearch.

The topics we will cover include the following:

- ML model deployment tuning techniques
- Estimating vector capacity for an Elasticsearch node
- Load testing with Elastic's performance tool, Rally
- Troubleshooting slow **k-nearest neighbor (kNN)** search response times

By the end of this chapter, you will understand how to estimate the number of Elasticsearch nodes required for your use case, how to use performance benchmarking to ensure those estimates are in line with your requirements, and identify potential causes for slow kNN search response times.

Let's begin by deploying a **natural language processing (NLP)** model.

Deploying an NLP model

Deploying an NLP model requires selecting a deployment method that can handle the expected inference load during peak production while being efficient and secure. During the testing phase, the model can often be run locally if it is small enough. However, a production use case necessitates a production deployment strategy. The model can be deployed on virtual machines, through a cloud provider service, on a dedicated model hosting service such as Hugging Face, or, when possible, within the same service where the vectors will be used, such as Elasticsearch. Each method has its trade-offs between efficiency, latency, scaling, and management.

Interaction with external deployment methods typically involves using APIs to send text inputs and receive vectors as outputs. Regardless of how the vectors are generated, they are sent to a data store for storage and can later be searched against using exact match or approximate nearest neighbor search. Vectors generated at query time are used to search across previously stored vectors.

Tuning deployed models for optimal performance and efficiency may involve making adjustments to factors such as hardware resources, software configurations, and model parameters. However, specific tuning guidelines are outside the scope of this book.

When deploying an embedding model in Elasticsearch, the model runs on dedicated ML nodes within the Elasticsearch cluster. This allows for seamless integration of the model with Elasticsearch's search and indexing capabilities. We'll cover some of the deployment tuning settings next.

Loading a model into Elasticsearch

Elasticsearch version 8.0+ has native support for `libtorch`, the C++ library used in `pytorch`. This allows it to run PyTorch-based models and generate embeddings within the stack.

To load a model into Elasticsearch, we will use the Eland Python library, as discussed in the previous chapter. Eland supports loading a model or supported architecture from your local drive, but the simplest way is to load a model from Hugging Face. The documentation covers what types of models are currently supported: `https://www.elastic.co/guide/en/machine-learning/current/ml-nlp-model-ref.html`.

In the following example, we will load the `sentence-transformers/msmarco-MiniLM-L-12-v3` (`https://huggingface.co/sentence-transformers/msmarco-MiniLM-L-12-v3`) model directly from Hugging Face using Eland. Eland will download the model and chunk it up for loading into Elasticsearch.

In the previous chapter, we covered how to load an NLP model into a Jupyter Notebook using Python. As a reminder, you can view the Python code for working with Eland in the `chapter 3` folder of this book's GitHub repository: `https://github.com/PacktPublishing/Vector-Search-for-Practitioners-with-Elastic/tree/main/chapter3`.

Alternatively, you can use Eland with **Docker** if all you need is to use it to load a model. Docker is an open source platform that automates the deployment of applications inside lightweight and portable containers. It ensures that software runs reliably when moved from one computing environment to another. It is used to streamline the development process by creating, deploying, and running applications by using containers, which allow developers to package an application with all its dependencies into a standardized unit for software development. For more information on installing and using Docker, visit www.docker.com.

The Eland Docker container (a standardized, encapsulated environment that runs applications and their dependencies isolated from the underlying system and other containers) can be downloaded from the Eland GitHub repository: `https://github.com/elastic/eland`.

To install a model from Hugging Face using Docker, you can run the following command:

```
$ docker run -it --rm --network host \
    elastic/eland \
    eland_import_hub_model \
    --url http://host.docker.internal:9200/ \
    --hub-model-id sentence-transformers/msmarco-MiniLM-L-12-v3\
    --task-type ner
```

With the model loaded, let's take a look at how to deploy it, and what options we have for configuration.

Model deployment configurations

Once the model has been loaded into Elasticsearch, it must be deployed or started. Models run on nodes of the `ml` node type, as is the case when deploying in Elastic Cloud.

NLP models, such as embedding models, can be scaled to handle the required production inference load by configuring the number of allocations and the threads per allocation:

- **Allocations**: Increasing the number of allocation settings when starting a model increases the amount of model allocations across all available ML nodes. Increasing the number of allocations will generally improve overall throughput. This setting can be increased or decreased even once a model has been started.

- **Threads per allocation**: Increasing the number of threads per allocation affects the number of CPU threads used by each instance of the model. Increasing this number generally improves the inference time of each request. This value can only be changed when a model is deployed.

The combination of the two settings must not exceed the number of available threads distributed across all available ML nodes. There is a point of diminishing returns when increasing these numbers. You should test with your particular workload to find the optimal settings:

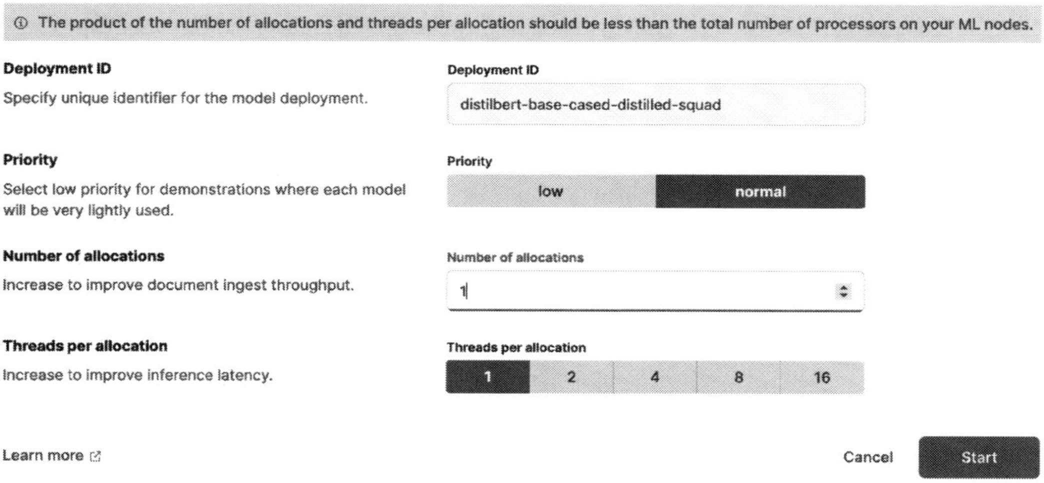

Figure 4.1: Model deployment settings

Loading the model will allow us to begin using it in performance testing before we move to a production setting. Let's look at the tool we have available to accomplish this.

Load testing

Benchmarking ingest and queries in Elasticsearch plays a crucial role in optimizing the performance of search and analytics operations. With Elasticsearch being widely used for handling large volumes of data, it is essential to ensure that both ingestion and query performance are as efficient as possible. To achieve this, it is necessary to identify bottlenecks and areas for improvement within the system. This can be done through a thorough process of benchmarking and performance testing, allowing users to identify and resolve any performance issues before they become critical.

Rally

Rally is a free benchmarking tool developed by Elastic that allows users to measure and optimize Elasticsearch performance. Rally can be used to benchmark various Elasticsearch operations, such as indexing, searching, and aggregating data. It is designed to support a wide range of scenarios and workloads, making it an ideal choice for users who want to ensure that their Elasticsearch clusters are running at peak performance. In this chapter, we will be focusing on using Rally to benchmark the performance of vector search in Elasticsearch, an essential aspect of many advanced search use cases.

Rally provides a set of tracks and datasets that represent various types of data, such as logging, metrics, security, and vectors. Users can use these provided tracks to benchmark a cluster as they make changes to configurations and/or version upgrades.

While there are many components to the Rally framework, the three main components we will be working with are as follows:

- **Track**: A track in Rally represents a series of benchmarks and workloads that simulate different operations (such as indexing or querying) against Elasticsearch

- **Race**: A race in Rally is an execution of a track, where the performance of Elasticsearch operations is measured under specific conditions

- **Challenge**: A challenge within Rally is a specific set of operations or tasks within a track, designed to test different aspects of Elasticsearch's performance under varying configurations and loads.

In Rally, a track defines the operations to be benchmarked, a challenge specifies the particular tasks and conditions under which the track is executed, and a race is the actual run of the challenge on the track to measure Elasticsearch's performance.

Users will get the most benefits when they take the time to create custom tracks with their data and configure Rally to use queries that are of the same structure so that they can used in production. One of the largest benefits provided by Rally is the ability to run repeatable tests as the user changes their data. This is especially useful early in the data cluster architecting phase to test how settings such as the number of shards and replicas and the number of docs on a single node will affect indexing speed and query response times.

Follow the download instructions for your environment, as outlined in the documentation at `https://esrally.readthedocs.io/en/stable/install.html`.

We will be using a vector track from Rally that's been specifically designed to benchmark advanced searches on dense vector fields. This track, known as the StackOverflow vector track, is derived from a dataset of StackOverflow posts and contains a variety of fields, including dense vectors, to support advanced search features such as ANN with filtering and hybrid search. By using this vector track, we will be able to measure and optimize the performance of vector search in Elasticsearch and gain insights into the best practices for managing Elasticsearch clusters that handle high-dimensional vector data.

> **Note**
>
> By default, Rally will output a large set of metrics to a log file, but an Elasticsearch cluster can be configured to collect these results. The results can then be searched and visualized on a Kibana dashboard so that you can compare tests.

Now that we know what Rally does, let's learn how to run it.

Setting up our Python environment to run Rally

In this section, we will provide code snippets and descriptions that you can use as examples. You can copy and run these examples to follow along with the benchmarking process:

1. Create a Python virtual environment:

```
sudo apt-get install python3-venv
python3 -m venv rally_testing
source rally_testing/bin/activate
pip install --upgrade pip
```

2. Install the necessary dependencies and packages:

```
sudo apt-get install gcc libffi-dev python3-dev
pip install elasticsearch
```

3. Install Rally and the StackOverflow track:

```
pip install esrally
esrally --version
esrally list tracks
```

Now that we've set up our Python environment to run Rally, let's see how to configure Rally.

Configuring Rally

Next up, we will configure Rally to send metrics to an Elasticsearch cluster. The best practice is to send metrics to a separate cluster from the one you are benchmarking.

All the available options for reporting can be found in the documentation: https://esrally.readthedocs.io/en/stable/configuration.html?highlight=reporting#reporting.

Open the rally.ini file in a text editor of choice and modify the [reporting] section. When you are done editing, the .ini file should look as follows. This example is connecting to a dedicated monitoring cluster in Elastic Cloud. A **monitoring cluster** allows you to collect reporting metrics over time:

```
vim ~/.rally/rally.ini
[reporting]
datastore.type = elasticsearch
datastore.host = my_monitoring_cluster.es.us-central1.gcp.cloud.es.io
datastore.port = 9243
datastore.secure = true
datastore.user = rally
datastore.password = rally_password
```

With Rally configured, let's move on to benchmarking our Elasticsearch cluster.

Running a race on an existing cluster

We will be benchmarking an existing Elasticsearch test cluster to ensure our test Elasticsearch cluster is configured the way we need it for the test. We will pass the track information and test cluster information on the command line.

> **Warning**
>
> Do not benchmark a production cluster! Benchmarking is designed to find the limits of performance and can cause slowdowns in normal operations. This is expected when testing but it can affect the performance of a production environment where performance is critical to business operations.

More information can be found in the Rally docs: `https://esrally.readthedocs.io/en/stable/recipes.html#benchmarking-an-existing-cluster`.

Let's break down the arguments for `esrally`:

- `race`: This tells `esrally` we will run a race
- `--track`: This defines the track we will use
- `--target-hosts`: This specifies which hosts we will run against – in this case, a test cluster in Elastic Cloud
- `--pipeline=benchmark-only`: This tells `esrally` not to create a new cluster and to use an existing one
- `--client-options`: This specifies the required options when security is enabled

Executing all these arguments with `esrally` looks like this:

```
esrally race --track=so_vector --target-hosts=deployment_name.
es.us-central1.gcp.cloud.es.io:9243 --pipeline=benchmark-
only --track-params ingest_percentage:100 --client-options="use_
ssl:true,verify_certs:true,basic_auth_user:'elastic',basic_auth_
password:'elastic_password'"
```

Please note that the `so_vector` track is over 32 GB in size.

Rally will start to run. It will download the track data if it has not been downloaded already.

Now that we understand how to run Rally, the next step is to get an Elasticsearch node ready for testing. To do that, we need to estimate how many vectors will "fit" on a single node.

RAM estimation

For kNN search to be performant, vectors need to "fit" in off-heap RAM on the data nodes. See the kNN performance tuning documentation for more information: `https://www.elastic.co/guide/en/elasticsearch/reference/current/tune-knn-search.html#_ensure_data_nodes_have_enough_memory`.

As of Elasticsearch version 8.7+, the rough estimate required for vectors is as follows:

```
num_vectors * 4 * (num_dimensions + 12)
```

Let's take a closer look:

- num_vectors: This is the count of individual vector fields. If you have 9 million documents and 1 vector per doc, the count would be 9 million. If you have 1 replica, then the count would be 18 million.

- num_dimensions: This is the number of dimensions the embedding model generates.

Note that this formula applies to float-type vectors only.

As an example, with 9 million vector fields, one per document, we would have the following:

```
9000000*4*(768 +12) =~ 26.2GB of RAM
```

This gives us a starting estimate of 26 GB of RAM (off-heap from the Elasticsearch JVM) required across the data nodes for performant kNN search. Note that each replica that's added requires the same amount of additional RAM. A standard Elasticsearch node is set up with the JVM taking half the available RAM. So, we are estimating that a standard 64 GB Elastic Cloud data node should be able to handle keeping 9 million 768 dimension vectors in cache. But we need to test this to confirm that this is the case!

With our estimate in place, we can begin the benchmarking process.

Benchmarking vector search

As mentioned previously, Rally is a full-performance benchmarking tool with many uses and advanced configurations. Covering them all would take a book of its own, so we will just provide a high-level overview here. Rally has extensive documentation at `https://esrally.readthedocs.io`.

When using Rally to benchmark vector search, especially kNN search, the approach is fairly straightforward but intentionally methodical:

1. Start with a single full-sized node, such as a VM of 60 GB or 64 GB or RAM. By default, the Elasticsearch JVM will take half, but you can also experiment by configuring 16 GB JVM heaps.

2. Configure a test index to have a single primary shard and zero replicas.

3. Using the RAM calculation discussed previously, index 60% of the estimated vectors into the single node.

4. Run Rally with a custom track configured only for the search querying.

5. Analyze the results while taking note of **service time** and **latency**:

    *   Service time is the time to run the actual query in Elasticsearch.

    *   Latency is the full time from Rally putting the query in line to finishing the task. You normally want low latency.

6. Load an additional 10% of the documents into the cluster.

7. Repeat the Rally test and analyze the results.

8. If the times stay consistent, continue slowly loading documents and rerunning Rally until the metrics dramatically increase.

9. When the response times spike, you can consider the previous "good" run's document count to be close to a full-sized node's capacity to hold vectors in RAM.

10. You can confirm this by running GET /_nodes/hot_threads (discussed later in this chapter).

You will need to test with this methodology to determine the maximum number of vectors that can "fit" in off-heap RAM. However, it is important to keep in mind that the standard Elasticsearch 10 to 50 GB per shared guidance still applies as searching a single shard is, at the time of writing, still single-threaded.

More primary shards can potentially improve indexing time by spreading the incoming documents across more data nodes (if they exist). With fast search response time requirements, aiming for the lower end of the shard sizing recommendation has often been found to give the best performance.

Evaluating results

In this section, we'll look at some example test runs that use the following values:

*   The cohere_vector rally track with default settings: github.com/elastic/rally-tracks/tree/master/cohere_vector

*   Vectors that are 768-dimension float32

*   One hot node with 64 GM of RAM using the DATAHOT.N2.68X10X45 Elastic Cloud configuration

*   Working off the rough calculation that 11 million vectors would take roughly 32 GB of RAM in 8.10.3 Elasticsearch

Each use case has its own set of requirements. An "acceptable" response time must also be decided by considering factors such as the following:

*   How the data is used – external users, internal users, programmatic querying

- Data sizes to be queried

- Budget

These are just a few examples. These all come into play when you're deciding what response time must be achieved for a project.

For our testing example, we are shooting for a response time of less than 300 milliseconds. This test was designed to help you understand the performance of a single node before we scale out to a multi-node production cluster.

Testing with 7.2 million vectors

The response time here is deemed acceptable:

```
| 50th percentile service time | standalone-knn-search-100-1000-
single-client |    63.2092 | ms |
| 90th percentile service time | standalone-knn-search-100-1000-
single-client |    70.9459 | ms |
| 100th percentile service time | standalone-knn-search-100-1000-
single-client |   204.182  | ms |
```

Testing with 9 million vectors

The response time here is still deemed acceptable:

```
| 50th percentile service time  | standalone-knn-search-100-1000-
single-client |    63.3707  | ms |
| 90th percentile service time  | standalone-knn-search-100-1000-
single-client |    71.7568  | ms |
| 100th percentile service time | standalone-knn-search-100-1000-
single-client |   303.927   | ms |
```

Testing with 13.8 million vectors

Here, we can see the service time spike above acceptable values for the sample use case. This is most likely due to the size of vectors exceeding the available off-heap RAM, causing kNN search response times to significantly increase:

```
| 50th percentile service time  |    standalone-knn-search-100-1000-
single-client |    763.32  |    ms |
| 90th percentile service time  |    standalone-knn-search-100-1000-
single-client |   1045.13  |    ms |
| 100th percentile service time |    standalone-knn-search-100-1000-
single-client |   1655.94  |    ms |
```

In this case, we would say a single node's dense vector capacity (for kNN search) is around 10 million.

Working from this number, we can begin to scale out the number of nodes and add additional replicas as needed.

Troubleshooting slowdown

We have identified our single-node approximate capacity to cache and run our vectors, but it can be helpful to look at other indicators to check or confirm why slowdowns may be happening.

When slowdowns occur with kNN search, it is often related to not having enough off-heap RAM. Let's look at additional methods to help us diagnose the issue.

Hot Threads API

The Hot Threads API in Elasticsearch helps identify slow-performing components by providing information about the busiest threads across all nodes or specific nodes in the cluster. Analyzing the output of the Hot Threads API can help diagnose performance bottlenecks and slowdowns. Let's learn how to analyze the Hot Threads API's output.

Use the Hot Threads API to get the details of the busiest threads. The API can be accessed using the following endpoint:

```
GET /_nodes/hot_threads
```

You can also target specific nodes or customize the output by specifying additional parameters, such as the number of threads to return or the interval between snapshots:

```
GET /_nodes/{nodeId}/hot_threads?threads=3&interval=500ms&snapshots=5
```

The API's output consists of stack traces for the busiest threads. Generally, you start by looking for patterns or recurring themes in these stack traces to identify the source of the slowdown. Common issues might include heavy garbage collection, slow or complex queries, shard rebalancing, or resource-intensive aggregations.

When specifically troubleshooting slowdowns with kNN search, we start by looking for threads related to the Hierarchical Navigable Small World (HNSW). An example of one such thread (partial) is as follows:

```
100.0% [cpu=4.7%, other=95.3%] (500ms out of 500ms) cpu usage by
thread 'elasticsearch[instance-0000000020][search][T#8]'
     2/10 snapshots sharing following 33 elements
        app//org.apache.lucene.codecs.lucene91.
Lucene91HnswVectorsReader$OffHeapVectorValues.
vectorValue(Lucene91HnswVectorsReader.java:499)
        app//org.apache.lucene.util.hnsw.HnswGraphSearcher.
searchLevel(HnswGraphSearcher.java:182)
```

In this stack trace, we can see the following:

- Most time is spent on other (95.3%) rather than cpu (4.7%)

- When we look at what code is being run, we
  see Lucene91HnswVectorsReader$OffHeapVectorValues

These two pieces of information give us a strong indication that slowdowns are being caused, at least partly, by Lucene having to retrieve vectors from disk rather than from the page cache. The key point here is that the low `cpu` percentage and high `other` percentage indicate it is waiting as it reads vectors from disk.

However, note that most or all of the percentage is in `cpu` and not `other`, that is most likely expected.

Another excellent indicator to watch is major page faults.

Major page faults

Monitoring the major page faults metric can help indicate that Elasticsearch has to read vectors from disk.

A major page fault in Linux occurs when the operating system needs to fetch data from the disk to fulfill a program's request for memory access. This happens when the requested memory page is not currently loaded in the system's RAM.

This process is called a major page fault as it takes longer than a minor page fault, where the requested data is already present in the memory but not yet mapped to the program's address space. Since disk access is much slower than memory access, major page faults can negatively impact a program's performance.

Elastic's Metricbeat is a lightweight shipper that you can install on your servers to periodically collect metrics from the operating system and services running on the server. Its system module can collect major page fault values (`https://www.elastic.co/guide/en/beats/metricbeat/current/metricbeat-metricset-system-process.html`).

This data can be charted in Kibana, the visualization application for Elasticsearch. Major page faults during the kNN search indicate some of the vectors were not able to be stored in the page cache and had to be loaded from disk. Monitoring this metric along with `hot_threads` gives the best indication that more off-heap RAM is needed for a performant kNN search:

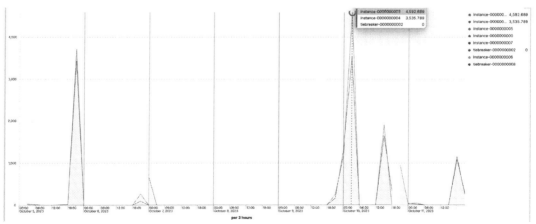

Figure 4.2: Major page faults per Elasticsearch node in 3-hour buckets
(The textual detail in the above figure is minimized and is not directly relevant for the display
of the graphic. Please refer to the Free eBook download to access the detail in the graphic.)

Zooming in on the largest spike, we can see that the page faults for instance 3 are above 4,592 for 4 hours. This is much higher than what we would normally want to see:

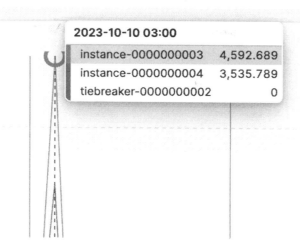

Figure 4.3: A zoomed-in view of the major page faults chart

Hot Threads and Major Page Faults are helpful tools for diagnosing search slowdowns. At indexing time, there are a few items to consider.

Indexing considerations

The following are some aspects you should consider:

- Concurrent searches are supported, but heavy indexing can make searches slower. This is because indexing can steal computing resources from search. It can also cause many small segments to be created, which is not good for search performance.

- In general, we recommend separating active indexing/updates from search as much as possible. So, if you need to reindex to update the vector embedding, that should be done in a separate index (or better yet, a separate cluster) rather than in-place. Alternatively, you could reindex at off-peak hours, such as overnight (assuming there are off-peak hours).

- Prefer fewer `_bulk` requests but with more vectors in them.

- Make fewer requests to the server.

- Start with 10 MB bulk and tune from there.

Summary

In this chapter, you delved into the nuances of optimizing vector search performance in Elasticsearch. We explored various tuning techniques, highlighting the intricacies of ML model deployment, node scaling, and configuration tuning. Tools such as Rally were introduced to aid in load testing specific use cases. Moreover, the focus on troubleshooting – bolstered by insights into monitoring cluster metrics and the hot threads API – has empowered you with the skills to tackle slow queries effectively.

In the next chapter, we will shift from text-focused semantic search to image-focused semantic search and explore the history and practical uses for these models, expanding our vector search capabilities.

Part 3: Specialized Use Cases

This section delves into the specialized applications of vector search across various domains. From image search to the intricacies of cybersecurity, it explores how vector search is uniquely adapted to different contexts. These chapters provide a detailed perspective on the versatility of vector search, demonstrating its wide-ranging impact and utility in addressing specific, industry-related challenges.

This part has the following chapters:

- *Chapter 5, Image Search*
- *Chapter 6, Redacting Personal Identifiable Information Using Elasticsearch*
- *Chapter 7, Next Generation of Observability Powered by Vectors*
- *Chapter 8, The Power of Vectors and Embedding in Bolstering Cybersecurity*

5
Image Search

In this chapter, we will explore the techniques involved in similarity search with images. We will discuss the evolution of image search over recent years and delve into the mechanism behind image search. As similarity search continues to expand in the world of search today, it is becoming an integral part of what users come to expect.

We will cover the following concepts:

- An overview of image search
- The role of vector search with images
- Creating a vector representation of an image, storing it in Elasticsearch, and performing a kNN search using a source image
- Practical use cases for image and multimedia search today

Overview of image search

Image search is a specialized data retrieval methodology that focuses on finding images through the analysis and comparison of their visual content. The demand for effective image search technology has grown exponentially over the last few years due to an explosion in digital imagery across the internet, social media, and other digital platforms.

The evolution of image search

The origins of image search can be traced back to the early days of the internet when search engines could only analyze text associated with an image, such as filenames, alt text, or surrounding textual content, to match search queries. However, these methods had their limitations, as the actual content of images remained largely ignored.

With advancements in **artificial intelligence (AI)** and **machine learning (ML)**, the capabilities of image search have greatly expanded. Now, modern image search technology can analyze the actual visual content of images, thanks to the development of techniques such as **Convolutional Neural Networks (CNNs)**, image feature extraction, **Vision Transformers (VIT)**, and vector similarity search.

The mechanism behind image search

In the context of machine learning, an image can be understood as a matrix of pixel values, and these values can be used as features for machine learning models. To make this data manageable, techniques such as **dimensionality reduction** (covered in *Chapter 3, Model Management and Vector Considerations in Elastic*) and **feature extraction** are employed.

Dimensionality reduction refers to techniques that transform high-dimensional image data into lower-dimensional image data—preserving the most significant patterns or structures, to facilitate more efficient processing and analysis. Ideally, without a substantial loss of information. The goal of dimensionality reduction is faster computations and improving overall model performance.

Feature extraction involves processing an image to identify and describe distinct characteristics, such as edges, colors, or shapes. These features can then be used as input for machine learning algorithms.

One popular method for feature extraction in image search is the use of deep learning models, specifically CNNs. These models are designed to automatically and adaptively learn spatial hierarchies of features from images, which has proven highly effective in tasks such as image classification and object detection.

Once features are extracted from images, they are typically transformed into a vector representation that can be easily compared for similarity. This process is often referred to as **vectorization**. Each vector represents a point in a multi-dimensional space, and the "distance" between these points can be calculated to determine the similarity between images. The shorter the distance, the more similar the images are.

By understanding the essence of each image through vector representation, systems can rapidly sift through vast databases to pinpoint the most similar matches to a query. In essence, vector similarity search is the mechanism that empowers robust and efficient image-based search experiences.

The role of vector similarity search

Vector similarity search plays a crucial role in image search. After images are transformed into vectors, a search query (also represented as a vector) is compared against the database of image vectors to find the most similar matches. This process is known as **k-Nearest Neighbor (kNN)** search, where "k" represents the number of similar items to retrieve.

Several algorithms can be used for kNN search, including **brute-force search** and more efficient methods such as the **Hierarchical Navigable Small World (HNSW)** algorithm (see *Chapter 7, Next Generation of Observability Powered, by Vectors* for a more in-depth discussion on HNSW). Brute-force search involves comparing the query vector with every vector in the database, which can be computationally expensive for large databases. On the other hand, HNSW is an optimized algorithm that can quickly find the nearest neighbors in a large-scale database, making it particularly useful for vector similarity search in image search systems.

The tangible benefits of image search are observed across industries. Its flexibility and adaptability make it a tool of choice for enhancing user experiences, ensuring digital security, or even revolutionizing digital content interactions.

Image search in practice

Applications of image search are varied and far-reaching. In e-commerce, for example, reverse image search allows customers to upload a photo of a product and find similar items for sale. In the field of digital forensics, image search can be used to find visually similar images across a database to detect illicit content. It is also used in the realm of social media for face recognition, image tagging, and content recommendation.

As we continue to generate and share more visual content, the need for effective and efficient image search technology will only grow. The combination of artificial intelligence, machine learning, and vector similarity search provides a powerful toolkit to meet this demand, powering a new generation of image search capabilities that can analyze and understand visual content.

Traditionally, image search engines use text-based metadata associated with images, such as the image's filename, alt text, and surrounding text context, to understand the content of an image. This approach, however, is limited by the accuracy and completeness of the metadata, and it fails to analyze the actual visual content of the image itself.

Over time, with advancements in artificial intelligence and machine learning, more sophisticated methods of image search have been developed that can analyze the visual content of images directly. This technique, known as **content-based image retrieval** (**CBIR**), involves extracting **feature vectors** from images and using these vectors to find visually similar images.

Feature vectors are a numerical representation of an image's visual content. They are generated by applying a feature extraction algorithm to the image. The specifics of the feature extraction process can vary, but in general, it involves analyzing the image's colors, textures, and shapes. In recent years, CNNs have become a popular tool for feature extraction due to their ability to capture complex patterns in image data.

Once feature vectors have been extracted from a set of images, these vectors can be indexed in a database. When a new query image is submitted, its feature vector is compared to the indexed vectors, and the images with the most similar vectors are returned as the search results. The similarity between vectors is typically measured using distance metrics such as **Euclidean distance** or **cosine similarity**.

Despite the impressive capabilities of CBIR systems, there are several challenges in implementing them. For instance, interpreting and understanding the semantic meaning of images is a complex task due to the subjective nature of visual perception. Furthermore, the high dimensionality of image data can make the search process computationally expensive, particularly for large databases.

To address these challenges, **approximate nearest neighbor** (**ANN**) search algorithms, such as the HNSW graph, are often used to optimize the search process. These algorithms sacrifice a small amount of accuracy for a significant increase in search speed, making them a practical choice for large-scale image search applications.

With the advent of Elasticsearch's dense vector field type, it is now possible to index and search high-dimensional vectors directly within an Elasticsearch cluster. This functionality, combined with an appropriate feature extraction model, provides a powerful toolset for building efficient and scalable image search systems.

In the following sections, we will delve into the details of image feature extraction, vector indexing, and search techniques. We will also demonstrate how to implement an image search system using Elasticsearch and a pre-trained CNN model for feature extraction. The overarching goal is to provide a comprehensive guide for building and optimizing image search systems using state-of-the-art technology.

Vector search with images

Vector search is a transformative feature of Elasticsearch and other vector stores that enables a method for performing searches within complex data types such as images. Through this approach, images are converted into vectors that can be indexed, searched, and compared against each other, revolutionizing the way we can retrieve and analyze image data. This inherent characteristic of producing embeddings applies to other media types as well. This section provides an in-depth overview of the vector search process with images, including image vectorization, vector indexing in Elasticsearch, kNN search, vector similarity metrics, and fine-tuning the kNN algorithm.

Image vectorization

The first phase of the vector search process involves transforming the image data into a vector, a process known as image vectorization. Deep learning models, specifically CNNs, are typically employed for this task. CNNs are designed to understand and capture the intricate features of an image, such as color distribution, shapes, textures, and patterns. By processing an image through layers of convolutional, pooling, and fully connected nodes, a CNN can represent an image as a high-dimensional vector. This vector encapsulates the key features of the image, serving as its numerical representation.

The output layer of a pre-trained CNN (often referred to as an embedding or feature vector) is often used for this purpose. Each dimension in this vector represents some learned feature from the image. For instance, one dimension might correspond to the presence of a particular color or texture pattern. The values in the vector quantify the extent to which these features are present in the image.

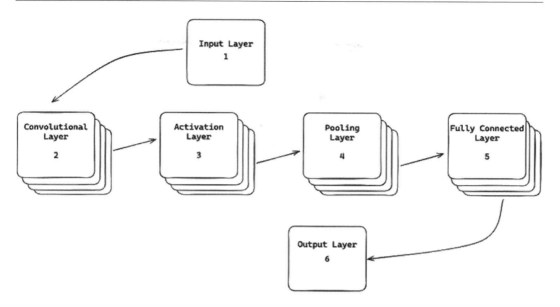

Figure 5.1: Layers of a CNN model

As seen in the preceding diagram, these are the layers of a CNN model:

1. Accepts raw pixel values of the image as input.

2. Each layer extracts specific features such as edges, corners, textures, and so on.

3. Introduces non-linearity, learns from errors, and approximates more complex functions.

4. Reduces the dimensions of feature maps through down-sampling to decrease the computational complexity.

5. Consists of the weights and biases from the previous layers for the classification process to take place.

6. Outputs a probability distribution over classes.

Indexing image vectors in Elasticsearch

Once the image vectors have been obtained, the next step is to index these vectors in Elasticsearch for future searching. Elasticsearch provides a special field type, the dense_vector field, to handle the storage of these high-dimensional vectors.

A dense_vector field is defined as an array of numeric values, typically floating-point numbers, with a specified number of dimensions (dims). The maximum number of dimensions allowed for indexed vectors is currently 2,048, though this may be further increased in the future. It's essential to note that each dense_vector field is single-valued, meaning that it is not possible to store multiple values in one such field.

In the context of image search, each image (now represented as a vector) is indexed into an Elasticsearch document. This vector can be one per document or multiple vectors per document. The vector representing the image is stored in a `dense_vector` field within the document. Additionally, other relevant information or metadata about the image can be stored in other fields within the same document.

The full example code can be found in the Jupyter Notebook available in the `chapter 5` folder of this book's GitHub repository at `https://github.com/PacktPublishing/Vector-Search-for-Practitioners-with-Elastic/tree/main/chapter5`, but we'll discuss the relevant parts here.

First, we will initialize a pre-trained model using the `SentenceTransformer` library.

The `clip-ViT-B-32-multilingual-v1` model is discussed in detail later in this chapter:

```
model = SentenceTransformer('clip-ViT-B-32-multilingual-v1')
```

Next, we will prepare the image transformation function:

```
transform = transforms.Compose([
    transforms.Resize(224),
    transforms.CenterCrop(224),
    lambda image: image.convert("RGB"),
    transforms.ToTensor(),
    transforms.Normalize((0.5, 0.5, 0.5), (0.5, 0.5, 0.5)),
])
```

`Transforms.Compose()` combines all the following transformations:

- `transforms.Resize(224)`: Resizes the shorter side of the image to 224 pixels while maintaining the aspect ratio.

- `transforms.CenterCrop(224)`: Crops the center of the image so that the resultant image has dimensions of 224x224 pixels.

- `lambda image: image.convert("RGB")`: This is a transformation that converts the image to the RGB format. This is useful for grayscale images or images with an alpha channel, as deep learning models typically expect RGB inputs.

- `transforms.ToTensor()`: Converts the image (in the PIL image format) into a PyTorch tensor. This will change the data from a range of [0, 255] in the PIL image format to a float in a range [0.0, 1.0].

- `transforms.Normalize((0.5, 0.5, 0.5), (0.5, 0.5, 0.5))`: Normalizes the tensor image with a given mean and standard deviation for each channel. In this case, the mean and standard deviation for all three channels (R, G, B) are 0.5. This normalization will transform the data range from [0.0, 1.0] to [-1.0, 1.0].

We can use the following code to apply the transform to an image file and then generate an image vector using the model. See the Python notebook for this chapter to run against actual image files:

```python
from PIL import Image
img = Image.open("image_file.jpg")
image = transform(img).unsqueeze(0)
image_vector = model.encode(image)
```

The vector and other associated data can then be indexed into Elasticsearch for use with kNN search:

```python
# Create document
    document = {'_index': index_name,
                '_source': {"filename": filename,
                            "image_vector": vector
```

See the complete code in the chapter 5 folder of this book's GitHub repository.

With vectors generated and indexed into Elasticsearch, we can move on to searching for similar images.

k-Nearest Neighbor (kNN) search

With the vectors now indexed in Elasticsearch, the next step is to make use of kNN search. You can refer back to *Chapter 2, Getting Started with Vector Search in Elastic*, for a full discussion on kNN and HNSW search.

As with text-based vector search, when performing vector search with images, we first need to convert our query image to a vector. The process is the same as we used to convert images to vectors at index time.

We convert the image to a vector and include that vector in the query_vector parameter of the knn search function:

```python
knn = {
    "field": "image_vector",
    "query_vector": search_image_vector[0],
    "k": 1,
    "num_candidates": 10
  }
```

Here, we specify the following:

- field: The field in the index that contains vector representations of images we are searching against

- query_vector: The vector representation of our query image

- k: We want only one closest image

- num_candidates: The number of approximate nearest neighbor candidates on each shard to search against

With an understanding of how to convert an image to a vector representation and perform an approximate nearest neighbor search, let's discuss some of the challenges.

Challenges and limitations with image search

While vector search with images offers powerful capabilities for image retrieval, it also comes with certain challenges and limitations. One of the main challenges is the high dimensionality of image vectors, which can lead to computational inefficiencies and difficulties in visualizing and interpreting the data.

Additionally, while pre-trained models for feature extraction can capture a wide range of features, they may not always align with the specific features that are relevant to a particular use case. This can lead to suboptimal search results. One potential solution, not limited to image search, is to use transfer learning to fine-tune the feature extraction model on a specific task, although this requires additional data and computational resources.

Multi-modal models for vector search

Combining text and image classification allows for a more comprehensive understanding of relationships between multiple types of data. We've generated vectors for our images and learned how to search for similar images, so let's explore what multi-modal vector search is and some practical use cases for it.

Introduction and rationale

The advent of multi-modal models has sparked a seismic shift in our understanding of data analysis and representation. Three examples where this innovative technology can be harnessed include news agencies, e-commerce websites, and social media platforms. Each of these sectors can significantly benefit from the versatility and adaptability of multimedia search, enhancing user experience and boosting their growth.

At their core, multi-modal models seek to integrate and interpret information from different types of data, such as text and images. This integrative approach allows these models to capture nuanced interactions between various data types, often yielding results that are greater than the sum of their parts. A powerful example of this synergy is the combination of text descriptions and image classifications within the same vector space.

The benefits of this approach are manifold. First, it greatly enhances search capabilities, as queries can now retrieve results based on text and visual information. For instance, a query about a "green apple" could return images of green apples, text descriptions of green apples, or a combination of both.

Second, this approach can significantly improve the relevance of search results. Since the model considers both textual and visual information, it has a broader and richer understanding of the queried concept. This richer understanding can help filter out irrelevant results and prioritize those that best match the query from different angles.

Lastly, this approach facilitates cross-modal search, such as text-to-image and image-to-text search. For example, a user can input a text query and receive image results, or vice versa. This expands the usability of the search system and makes it more flexible and user-friendly.

Understanding the concept of vector space in multi-modal models

The cornerstone of a multi-modal model's operation and its subsequent capabilities lies within its vector space, often denoted as a "shared" or "common" vector space. This concept, borrowed from linear algebra, forms the groundwork of how multi-modal models function, offering a platform where different types of data can be harmoniously represented and processed.

In this shared vector space, vectors—parametrized mathematical entities with both magnitude and direction—are used to represent different data modalities. This might include text descriptions and images that the model is working with. Each of these vectors then represents a point in the multi-dimensional space that corresponds to an individual text description or an image. This representation is both elegant and useful, as the geometric proximity or distance between two vectors can then be used to indicate the similarity or dissimilarity between two corresponding entities.

The notion of geometric proximity here is not arbitrary; it's grounded in the theory of metric spaces, where a distance function (or metric) quantifies the dissimilarity between any two objects within the space. In a multi-modal vector space, cosine similarity or Euclidean distance are commonly used as metrics. The lower the distance (or the higher the cosine similarity), the more similar the two vectors—and thus the two corresponding entities—are to each other.

To operationalize this idea, the model employs vectorization, discussed earlier in this chapter. During vectorization, the model converts, or encodes, text descriptions and images into vectors using two different encoders—one for text and another for images. This conversion is akin to a translation process, where the complexities and characteristics of text descriptions and images are distilled into the language of vectors, a language that the model can more readily understand, analyze, and learn from.

Unlike traditional computer vision models that require labeled image datasets, CLIP harnesses the vast number of text-image pairs available online to understand and categorize images in a flexible manner. This unique approach allows CLIP to generalize across a wide range of tasks without the need for task-specific fine-tuning, highlighting the power and potential of multi-modal models in bridging the gap between vision and language.

Introduction to the OpenAI clip-ViT-B-32-multilingual-v1 model

The **OpenAI clip-ViT-B-32-multilingual-v1 model**, commonly referred to as **CLIP**, is a shining example of a multi-modal model. Introduced on January 5, 2021, CLIP revolutionized the field of computer vision by learning visual concepts efficiently from natural language supervision (`openai.com/research/clip`). In other words, it was trained to recognize a wide variety of images based on a wide variety of text descriptions found on the internet.

Unlike most computer vision models that are trained on manually labeled datasets, CLIP was trained on text-image pairs that are readily available on the internet. This method of training allowed CLIP to learn a wide variety of visual concepts and their associated names, enabling it to perform a wide variety of classification tasks. CLIP's capabilities, however, are not without limitations. Its performance is dependent on the quality and diversity of the training data, and it may not perform well on tasks that require understanding nuanced visual details or context that was not adequately captured in the training data.

With the mechanics out of the way, let's explore some of the practical use cases for image vector search.

Implementing vector search for diverse media types

Now that we've understood the basics of multi-modal or multimedia search, let's delve a bit deeper into how it can be applied to various types of content:

- **Text**: Vector search can be used to find related documents, articles, or pieces of text. Each document is converted into a vector using techniques such as TF-IDF or word, sentence, or document embeddings. When a user enters a search query, the system finds the text vectors that are closest to the query vector.

- **Images**: Images can be analyzed using deep learning models to extract feature vectors. These vectors capture the visual content of the images. If a user searches with an image query, the system finds the image vectors that are most similar to the query image's vector.

- **Videos**: Videos are a bit more complex, as they contain both visual and audio information. However, similar techniques can be used to extract feature vectors from the video and audio content. The system then uses these vectors to find relevant videos in response to a user's query.

The power and potential of multimedia search truly shine when implemented in real-world scenarios.

News agencies

In the world of news agencies, multimedia search is a powerful tool for enhancing content discovery and providing a comprehensive news experience. Journalists, for instance, can benefit significantly from this technology. If they are writing about climate change, multimedia search can help them access a range of related content for their article. Not just related articles, but also images showing the effects of climate change, video clips of expert interviews, infographics illustrating climate trends, and even audio clips of speeches by climate activists. This broad range of multimedia content can enhance the depth and richness of their reporting. Additionally, from the consumer's perspective, multimedia search can curate a multimedia storyboard for readers, where related videos, infographics, photo galleries, and podcasts are presented alongside text articles, providing a richer, more immersive experience.

E-commerce platforms

E-commerce platforms can harness the power of multimedia search to take their product recommendations to the next level. By analyzing both text data such as product descriptions and customer reviews, and visual aspects of products through image recognition, they can offer more precise and personalized recommendations. For instance, if a user has been browsing vintage watches, the multimedia search algorithm could analyze the images of the watches viewed and understand the specific visual elements that attract the user. This analysis could then be used to recommend other products that share these visual features. This not only improves the accuracy of recommendations but also enhances the overall user experience, potentially leading to increased sales and customer retention.

Social media platforms

Social media platforms, teeming with multimedia content, can significantly benefit from multimedia search to improve content discovery and user engagement. Suppose a user posts a picture of a homemade pizza. In that case, multimedia search could analyze this image, recognize it as a pizza, and then suggest other related content – such as a video tutorial on pizza-making, blog posts about pizza recipes, or posts from other users who have also shared their homemade pizzas. This not only creates a more engaging and personalized social media experience but also enhances content moderation efforts. By analyzing the text, image, and video content, the platform can better detect and filter out inappropriate or harmful content, improving the overall quality and safety of the platform.

These integrated examples demonstrate the transformative potential of multimedia search across diverse sectors, from news agencies and e-commerce platforms to social media networks. By improving user engagement, enhancing content discovery, and personalization, multimedia search offers significant benefits that can revolutionize the way we interact with digital content.

These examples scratch the surface of the potential use cases for image and multimedia vector search. As models continue to advance and new industries begin to explore the possibilities, new use cases are being thought of each day.

Summary

In this chapter, our exploration of the world of similarity search with images provided us with an understanding of its evolution and practical workings. We discussed the transformative power of vector-based image search in today's fast-paced digital environment. We gained the ability to create vector representations of images and integrate them into Elasticsearch. We learned how harnessing the power of kNN search offers a myriad of possibilities for enhancing user experiences. We also saw how the applications of image and multimedia search span across numerous domains, solidifying its importance in the modern digital age.

In the next chapter, we will discuss how NLP models can be used, along with other Elasticsearch features, to redact personally identifiable information before it is ingested into Elasticsearch.

6

Redacting Personal Identifiable Information Using Elasticsearch

In this chapter, we will explore the process of creating and configuring a **Personal Identifiable Information (PII)** redaction pipeline in Elasticsearch to effectively identify and redact sensitive information from data. As data privacy and security become increasingly important, the ability to protect personal information is crucial for organizations.

We will cover the following:

- How to install and customize a PII redaction pipeline using Elasticsearch's ingest processors

- Expanding and enhancing the pipeline to meet your organization's specific data redaction needs

This process will empower you to create a robust, accurate, and efficient solution to safeguard sensitive information and ensure compliance with data privacy regulations.

Overview of PII and redaction

PII refers to any data that can be used to identify an individual, either directly or indirectly, when combined with other information. PII includes data such as names, addresses, phone numbers, email addresses, Social Security numbers, driver's license numbers, and credit card numbers. It is critical to protect PII due to privacy concerns, as well as legal and regulatory requirements that dictate how companies should manage and secure such data.

Redaction, in the context of data privacy, is the process of removing or obscuring sensitive information from documents, logs, and other data sources, so the remaining data can be shared or analyzed without exposing the PII. This involves techniques such as **masking**, **pseudonymization**, or **encryption**, depending on the context and requirements. The goal of redaction is to strike a balance between preserving the utility of the data and maintaining the privacy of the individuals involved.

Types of data that may contain PII

There are various types of data that may contain PII, and it is crucial to understand where sensitive information may reside within a company's systems. Four of the most common data types are the following:

- **Logs**: Logs generated by applications, servers, and other systems often contain PII. This can include user authentication data, IP addresses, user-generated content, or error messages that may inadvertently include sensitive information. Logs are essential for troubleshooting, monitoring, and analyzing system performance, but they can also pose a risk if not properly managed.

- **Application Performance Monitoring (APM) data**: APM tools help businesses monitor and manage the performance of their applications, often by capturing data about user interactions, system performance, and errors. This data can inadvertently include PII, such as usernames, email addresses, and even payment information if not properly sanitized.

- **Databases and data stores**: Companies store vast amounts of information in databases and other data stores, including customer information, employee records, and transaction data. These repositories often hold large amounts of PII and are therefore subject to strict data protection regulations.

- **Unstructured data**: PII can also be found in unstructured data sources, such as emails, documents, images, and more. This can make identifying and redacting PII more challenging, as it requires more advanced techniques, such as natural language processing, to parse and understand the content.

Having highlighted the primary domains where PII may reside, it's imperative to delve deeper into the potential hazards associated with mishandling such sensitive information. Specifically, when it comes to logs, where PII can often be overlooked, understanding the risks is of utmost importance. Now, we'll address the complications and consequences of inadvertently storing PII in logs.

Risks of storing PII in logs

Storing PII in logs, APM data, and other data sources can have significant consequences for both businesses and individuals if not properly managed and secured. The risks include (but are not limited to) the following:

- **Financial fines and penalties**: Companies that fail to comply with data protection regulations, such as the **General Data Protection Regulation (GDPR)** or the **California Consumer Privacy Act (CCPA)**, can face severe fines and penalties. These fines can reach millions of dollars, depending on the severity of the violation and the size of the company.

- **Reputational damage**: Data breaches and privacy violations can damage a company's reputation and erode customer trust. In some cases, the fallout from such incidents can lead to a loss of business, a decline in stock prices, and even bankruptcy.

- **Legal and regulatory consequences**: Companies that fail to protect PII can be subject to lawsuits, regulatory actions, and other legal consequences. These can be costly and time-consuming, and in some cases, may even result in criminal charges for company executives.

- **Risks to individuals**: When PII is leaked or lost, it can have severe consequences for the affected individuals. They may face identity theft, financial loss, or other forms of harm, and may need to take steps to protect themselves and their assets.

Now that we understand the types of PII and the risks of storing PII, let's examine how PII data is often lost or exposed.

How PII is leaked or lost

PII can be leaked or lost through various means, some of which are unintentional, while others may be the result of malicious activity. Understanding these potential sources of data leakage is critical for companies to prevent and mitigate PII exposure. Some common ways in which PII is leaked or lost include the following:

- **Human error**: Mistakes made by employees or other individuals can result in PII being inadvertently exposed. This can include accidental sharing of sensitive data, misconfiguring security settings, or using weak passwords that are easily compromised.

- **Insider threats**: Employees or contractors with malicious intent can intentionally leak PII, often for personal gain or to cause harm to the company. This can involve stealing sensitive data or sabotaging systems to expose PII.

- **External attacks**: Cybercriminals and hackers often target companies to steal PII, which can then be sold on the dark web or used for identity theft or other nefarious purposes. These attacks can take the form of phishing scams, ransomware, or exploiting vulnerabilities in a company's systems.

- **Insecure storage and transmission**: Storing PII in unencrypted or otherwise insecure formats can increase the risk of data breaches. Similarly, transmitting sensitive data over unsecured channels can expose PII to interception by malicious actors.

- **Third-party breaches**: Companies often share PII with vendors, partners, or other third parties. If these organizations suffer a data breach, the PII provided by the company may be exposed, even if the company itself has taken appropriate security measures.

By understanding these potential sources of PII leakage and loss, companies can take steps to protect sensitive data, implement appropriate security measures, and minimize the risks associated with storing and processing PII. This includes implementing access controls, encrypting data both at rest and in transit, conducting regular security audits and vulnerability assessments, and providing training to employees on data privacy and security best practices.

Now that we've grasped the importance of recognizing the sources of PII and implementing rigorous security measures, the next logical step is to discuss the practical techniques for redacting such sensitive information. In the digital age, where structured and unstructured data often mingle, a blended approach using both NER models and regex patterns emerges as a robust solution. Let's explore how these tools can be harnessed effectively to safeguard PII.

Redacting PII with NER models and regex patterns

The process of redacting PII often requires a multi-faceted approach to ensure that sensitive data is accurately identified and removed from various data sources. Two key techniques used to redact PII are **Named Entity Recognition** (**NER**) models and **regular expressions** (**regex**) patterns. Combining these methods can help identify a broad range of PII types and ensure comprehensive data protection.

NER models

NER is a **Natural Language Processing** (**NLP**) technique used to identify and classify named entities, such as names of people, locations, organizations, and other specific information within text data. NER models can be particularly useful in redacting PII, as they can identify entities that do not follow a common pattern or structure. This enables the detection and redaction of less predictable PII types, which may be more difficult to identify using regex patterns alone.

Machine learning models, such as those based on **BERT** (**Bidirectional Encoder Representations from Transformers**), have demonstrated significant success in NER tasks. One such model is **dslim/bert-base-NER** from Hugging Face, which has been trained to identify a variety of named entities. By leveraging NER models such as these, organizations can efficiently identify and redact PII present in unstructured text data, such as emails, documents, and logs.

Regex patterns

Regex are a powerful tool for pattern matching and manipulation within text data. Regex patterns are particularly useful for identifying and redacting PII that follows standard patterns or structures. By designing regex patterns to match these common structures, organizations can quickly and accurately detect and remove PII from various data sources.

Grok patterns offer a more user-friendly alternative to regex for pattern matching in text data. Grok patterns are essentially a collection of predefined regex patterns, which can be combined and reused to create more complex expressions with greater ease. This approach simplifies the process of writing and maintaining pattern-matching rules, making it more accessible to users who may not be well-versed in regex syntax.

For the redaction pipeline in Elasticsearch, we will be using a new processor called the **redact** processor. This processor utilizes Grok patterns rather than traditional regex for pattern matching. In the following section, we will discuss the implementation and usage of the redact processor in more detail, outlining how it leverages Grok patterns to identify and redact PII from data sources.

Examples of PII types that can be identified using regex/grok patterns include the following:

- **Credit card numbers**: Credit card numbers typically follow a specific pattern, with a fixed number of digits and recognizable formatting. Regex patterns can be designed to identify and redact these numbers, regardless of the card issuer.

- **Social Security numbers**: Social Security numbers in the United States consist of nine digits, separated into three groups by hyphens (e.g., 123-45-6789). This standard format makes it straightforward to create a regex pattern to identify and redact these numbers.

- **Bank account numbers**: While bank account numbers can vary in length and formatting depending on the financial institution, many banks follow a common pattern that can be identified using regex patterns. Additionally, the presence of specific keywords, such as "account number" or "routing number," can help refine regex patterns to accurately identify and redact this information.

- **Email addresses**: Email addresses follow a standard format with a local part, an "@" symbol, and a domain. Regex patterns can be designed to identify and redact email addresses, helping to protect the privacy of individuals and prevent potential data breaches.

- **Phone numbers**: Phone numbers often follow a recognizable pattern, with a fixed number of digits and standard formatting (e.g., (123) 456-7890 or +1 123 456 7890). Regex patterns can be used to identify and redact phone numbers from various data sources, ensuring that contact information remains private.

While grok patterns excel at recognizing structured data forms such as credit card numbers or email addresses, there remain subtle nuances in unstructured data that might elude them. Herein lies the value of merging grok with NER models. By integrating Grok's precision with the contextual depth of NER, we aim to create a more encompassing redaction strategy, significantly reducing the chances of PII going unnoticed. Let's explore this combined approach for more robust data protection.

Combining NER models and regex (or grok) patterns for PII redaction

To maximize the effectiveness of PII redaction, organizations should consider using a combination of NER models and regex patterns. This two-stage approach ensures that both structured and unstructured PII can be accurately identified and removed from data sources.

In the first stage, NER models can be applied to text data to identify named entities that may contain PII. The output from the NER models can then be used to redact or mask the identified entities within the text.

Having discussed the synergy of NER models with regex for spotting PII, let's discuss how to operationalize a PII redaction pipeline in Elasticsearch. The Elasticsearch platform offers a powerful solution with ingest pipelines, designed to scrub data upon ingestion. Melding the precision of grok patterns with our discussed techniques provides a more holistic approach to sensitive data handling.

PII redaction pipeline in Elasticsearch

The PII redaction pipeline in Elasticsearch aims to automatically redact sensitive information from data as it's ingested into the Elasticsearch cluster. This process ensures that sensitive data is protected, which is particularly important when handling personal information that could be used to identify an individual, such as names, addresses, phone numbers, and social security numbers.

In this section, we will discuss the steps users can take to configure the PII redaction pipeline in Elasticsearch.

For the complete code, open the Jupyter Notebook in the chapter 6 folder of the book's GitHub repository: https://github.com/PacktPublishing/Vector-Search-for-Practitioners-with-Elastic/tree/main/chapter6.

We will review the key points of the pipeline.

Generating synthetic PII

To run our pipeline, we will need a dataset. Thankfully we have faker, the Python library for generating fake data of a given type. Our task here involves two steps:

- Generating the data with faker
- Bulk-indexing the data in Elasticsearch

The following is the code to generate the data (you can use the pip install command to install Faker if not already installed):

```python
from faker import Faker
import json
from pprint import pprint

# Create an instance of the Faker class
fake = Faker()

# Define a function to generate fake personal identification
information
def generate_fake_pii(num_records):

fake_data = []

for x in range(num_records):
# Generate fake personal identification information
fn = fake.first_name()
ln = fake.last_name()
pn = fake.phone_number()
```

```
sn = fake.ssn()
ai = fake.random_element(elements=('active', 'inactive'))

call_log = {
'message' : f'{fn} {ln} called in from {pn}. Their account number is
{sn}',
'status' : ai
}

fake_data.append(call_log)
return fake_data

# Generate fake personal identification information for N individuals
num_records = 10 # Set the desired number of records
fake_pii_data = generate_fake_pii(num_records)

pprint(fake_pii_data)
```

This will output records that look like the following:

```
{
'message': 'Stephen Gomez called in from 9162417050. Their account
number is ' '275-51-8055',
'status': 'inactive'
},
# Import the required libraries
from faker import Faker
import json
# Create an instance of the Faker class
fake = Faker()
# Define a function to generate fake personal identification
information
def generate_fake_pii(num_records):
# Create an empty list to store the fake data
fake_data = []
# Generate the specified number of fake records
for _ in range(num_records):
# Generate fake personal identification information
person = {
    'first_name': fake.first_name(),
    'last_name': fake.last_name(),
    'email': fake.email(),
    'phone_number': fake.phone_number(),
```

```
        'address': fake.address(),
        'ssn': fake.ssn(),
        'birthdate': fake.date_of_birth(tzinfo=None, minimum_age=18,
maximum_age=90).strftime('%Y-%m-%d'),
        'gender': fake.random_element(elements=('M', 'F'))
    }
    # Append the fake data to the list
    fake_data.append(person)
    return fake_data


    # Generate fake personal identification information for N individuals
    num_records = 10 # Set the desired number of records here
    fake_pii_data = generate_fake_pii(num_records)
    print(fake_pii_data)
```

The preceding code allows you to set the desired number of documents to be generated. This dataset should have enough (fake) PII for you to test the redaction pipeline.

Once these test documents are generated, you can execute the second step, which will bulk index the documents into Elasticsearch:

```
from elasticsearch import Elasticsearch, helpers
# Bulk Indexer
# Define a function to generate an array of documents for
Elasticsearch
def generate_documents_array(fake_data, index_name):
# Create an empty list to store the documents
    documents = []
# Iterate over the fake data and format it as documents
    for person in fake_data:
# Create a document with the _index and _source keys
    document = {
        '_index': index_name,
        '_source': person
    }
# Append the document to the list of documents
    documents.append(document)
return documents
# Generate the array of documents for Elasticsearch
index_name = 'pii' # Set the desired index name here
documents_array = generate_documents_array(fake_pii_data, index_name)


# Initialize the Elasticsearch client
es = Elasticsearch(['HOSTNAME:PORT'],basic_auth=('USERNAME',
'PASSWORD'),verify_certs=False)
```

```
# Convert the bulk index body to a single string with newline
separators
print("Bulk request: ")
print(documents_array)

try:
        response = helpers.bulk(es, documents_array)
        print ("\nRESPONSE:", response)
except Exception as e:
        print("\nERROR:", e)
After running this code, you should see the following type of document
in the "pii" index in your Elasticsearch cluster:

{
            "_index": "pii",
            "_id": "Hzge9IcBeW7_RVqxfOjf",
            "_score": 1,
            "_source": {
                "first_name": "Jessica",
                "last_name": "Baker",
                "email": zrojas@example.com,
                "phone_number": "+1-537-947-4261",
                "address": """96702 Cannon Mall Serranofurt, KS
41609""",
                "ssn": "811-48-4463",
                "birthdate": "1977-10-30",
                "gender": "M"
            }
        }
```

With the fake data generated and indexed, we need to configure the default ingest pipeline and index template, and load the NER model.

Installing the default pipeline

To set up the PII redaction pipeline in Elasticsearch, we need to install the default pipeline and configure it to use the provided NER model from Hugging Face. The steps are as follows:

1. An ingest pipeline is a series of processors that are used to modify or enrich data before it's indexed in Elasticsearch. In the context of the PII redaction pipeline, the pipeline will be used to redact sensitive information from the data. To install the pipeline, you will need to copy the provided JSON example from the GitHub repository and create a new pipeline in Elasticsearch using this configuration.

You can use Elasticsearch's REST APIs to create the pipeline as follows:

```
PUT _ingest/pipeline/pii_redaction_pipeline
  {
  "description": "PII redacting ingest pipeline",
  "processors": [
      {
        "set": {
           "field": "redacted",
           "value": "{{{message}}}"
        }
      },
      {
        "inference": {
           "model_id": "dslim__bert-base-ner",
           "field_map": {
              "message": "text_field"
           }
        }
      },
      {
        "script": {
           "lang": "painless",
           "source": """String msg = ctx['message'];
        for (item in ctx['ml']['inference']['entities']) {
           msg = msg.replace(item['entity'], '<' + item['class_
name'] + '>')
        }
        ctx['redacted']=msg""",
           "if": "return ctx['ml']['inference']['entities'].
isEmpty() == false",
           "tag": "ner_redact",
           "description": "Redact NER entities"
        }
      },
      {
        "redact": {
           "field": "redacted",
           "patterns": [
              "%{PHONE:PHONE}",
              "%{SSN:SSN}"
           ],
           "pattern_definitions": {
              "SSN": """\d{3}-?\d{2}-?\d{4}""",
              "PHONE": """\d{3}-?\d{3}-?\d{4}"""
```

```
                    }
                }
            },
            {
                "remove": {
                    "field": [
                        "message",
                        "ml"
                    ]
                }
            }
        ],
        "on_failure": [
            {
                "set": {
                    "field": "failure",
                    "value": "pii_script-redact"
                }
            }
        ]
    }
}
```

2. Load and start the NER model from Hugging Face.

3. You will need to load a compatible NER model from the Hugging Face Model Hub using the eland library in Python. The model used in the example is dslim/bert-base-NER, but you can use any Elastic-compatible NER model.

4. To load and start the model, you can follow these steps:

```
# Install the necessary Python packages:
pip install eland elasticsearch transformers sentence_
transformers torch==1.13


#Import the required Python libraries:
from pathlib import Path
from eland.ml.pytorch import PyTorchModel
from eland.ml.pytorch.transformers import TransformerModel
from elasticsearch import Elasticsearch
from elasticsearch.client import MlClient
from elasticsearch.exceptions import NotFoundError


# Set up an Elasticsearch connection using your Elastic Cloud ID
and cluster-level API key:
es = Elasticsearch(cloud_id=es_cloud_id,
                           api_key=(es_api_id, es_api_key)
```

```
                                    )
es.info() # should return cluster info

# Download the model from Hugging Face and load it into
Elasticsearch:
hf_model_id='dslim/bert-base-NER'
tm = TransformerModel(model_id=hf_model_id, task_type="ner")'


es_model_id = tm.elasticsearch_model_id()
es_model_id

# Load the model into Elastic Cluster
# <Load the model using the provided Python code from the GitHub
repository>
```

5. Configure the inference processor to use the NER mode ID.

    The inference processor is responsible for running the NER model on the ingested data. You need to configure the processor to use the `model_id` of the NER model that you loaded in the previous step. In the JSON example of the ingest pipeline, you will find the following section:

```
{
   "inference": {
      "model_id": "dslim__bert-base-ner",
      "field_map": {
         "message": "text_field"
      }
   }
}
```

    Replace the `model_id` value ("dslim__bert-base-ner") with the actual `model_id` of the NER model that you've loaded into Elasticsearch.

6. After setting up the pipeline and the NER model, you will need to ensure that data ingested into your Elasticsearch index passes through the pipeline first. You can achieve this by specifying the pipeline as part of the indexing. Configure the data source or index settings so that the data going into the index is passed through the pipeline first. Review the documentation for an example of how to add an ingest pipeline to an indexing request (`https://www.elastic.co/guide/en/elasticsearch/reference/current/ingest.html#add-pipeline-to-indexing-request`).

With the ingest pipeline configured and the NER model loaded, we finally will configure the index template. The template defines the field data types as well as configuring data being written to the index to pass through the redaction pipeline.

The accompanying Python notebook has the complete Python code. We define the pipeline with the following setting:

```
"index.default_pipeline": "pii_redaction_pipeline_book"
```

The final step is using the Elasticsearch bulk index API to index the fake data and confirm that the sensitive data has been redacted.

After you complete this step, output documents should look similar to the following example:

```
{'_source':
  {
  'redacted': '<PER> called in from 001-<PHONE>x1311. Their account
number is <SSN>'
  'status': 'active'
  }
```

You'll notice the person's name, phone number, and **Social Security Number** (**SSN**) have been redacted.

Expected results

Once the PII redaction pipeline has been configured and set up in Elasticsearch, the expected results are as follows:

- When the NER model identifies an entity, that entity will be replaced with the corresponding entity type enclosed in angle brackets. For example, if the NER model identifies a person's name, it will be replaced with <PERSON>.

- When a regex pattern matches a value, that value will be replaced by the term <redacted>. This ensures that sensitive information, such as phone numbers and SSNs, is never visible in the processed data.

With our example PII redaction pipeline set up, let's look at how it can be further customized to fit an organization's specific needs.

Expanding and customizing options for the PII redaction pipeline in Elasticsearch

Ingest processors in Elasticsearch provide a powerful and flexible way to customize data processing and manipulation, which can be tailored to fit a company's individual PII data redaction needs. In this section, we will discuss several options for expanding and enhancing the default PII redaction pipeline to better serve specific use cases and requirements.

Customizing the default PII example

The default PII redaction pipeline provided in the example can easily be customized to better suit your organization's data and requirements. Some possible customizations include the following:

- **Replacing the example NER model with any other Elastic-compatible NER model**: The default pipeline uses the `dslim/bert-base-NER` model from Hugging Face, but you can replace it with any other Elastic-compatible NER model that better fits your specific needs.

- **Removing the NER model if this form of identification is not required**: If your data does not require NER-based identification, you can remove the NER model from the pipeline, simplifying the pipeline and potentially improving performance.

- **Easily modifying the regex/grok pattern step**: The pipeline uses regex/grok patterns to identify and redact specific patterns in the data, such as Social Security numbers and phone numbers. You can easily modify this step as follows:

  - **Adding new patterns when new PII sources are found or identified**: As new sources of PII are discovered or the data changes, you can add new regex/grok patterns to the pipeline to ensure that the new PII is correctly redacted.

  - **Modifying existing patterns to match patterns that may have passed through or been incorrectly matched**: If existing patterns are not working as expected, you can modify them to better match the data and improve the redaction process.

  - **Removing patterns when no longer needed or when not working as expected**: If certain patterns are no longer relevant or are causing issues, you can remove them from the pipeline to improve performance and reduce the chance of false positives.

Cloning the pipeline to create different versions for different data streams

Depending on your organization's data processing needs, you may require different redaction pipelines for different data streams. By cloning and customizing the default PII redaction pipeline, you can create multiple versions of the pipeline tailored to specific data sources or types, ensuring that the redaction process is accurate and efficient for each data stream.

Fine-tuning NER models for particular datasets

The default NER model provided in the example may not be ideal for every dataset or use case. Fine-tuning the NER model can improve the model's performance and accuracy for your specific data:

- **Identify PII entities specific to your data**: The default NER model is designed to recognize common entities such as names, organizations, and locations. However, your data may contain unique or industry-specific PII entities that the default model does not recognize. By fine-tuning the model on your data, you can improve its ability to identify and redact these specific PII entities.

  Examples of such entities could include medical record numbers, customer IDs, or other sensitive identifiers unique to your organization or industry.

- **General overview of fine-tuning**: Fine-tuning is the process of taking a pre-trained NER model and training it further on your specific data. This can result in a model that is better suited to your data and more accurately identifies and redacts PII.

The high-level process of fine-tuning a NER model typically involves the following steps:

I.   Collect and preprocess a labeled dataset containing examples of the PII entities you want the model to recognize.

II.   Split the labeled dataset into training and validation sets, ensuring that both sets contain a representative sample of the PII entities you want the model to recognize.

III. Fine-tune the pre-trained NER model on the training set, adjusting model parameters and hyperparameters as needed to achieve the best performance.

IV.   Regularly evaluate the model's performance on the validation set during the fine-tuning process to prevent overfitting and ensure that the model generalizes well to unseen data.

V.   Once the fine-tuning process is complete, evaluate the model's performance on a test set to confirm that it meets your organization's requirements for PII redaction accuracy and performance.

VI.   Integrate the fine-tuned model into your Elasticsearch PII redaction pipeline, replacing the default NER model.

Contextual awareness in PII redaction allows for more nuanced data protection. Instead of blanket redaction, the Elasticsearch PII redaction pipeline can be tailored to remove data based on its surrounding content. This ensures meaningful privacy measures without unnecessary data loss.

Logic for contextual awareness

In some cases, you may want to redact information only when it appears in specific contexts or is surrounded by certain words or phrases. For example, some organizations may not need to redact a phone number simply because it appears in a log message, but only when the phone number's owner's name appears in the same log message, thus connecting a phone number to a person. By adding custom logic to your PII redaction pipeline, you can ensure that the pipeline only triggers redaction under these specific conditions.

To implement contextual awareness in your PII redaction pipeline, consider the following steps:

1. Analyze your data and identify the contexts or surrounding words that should trigger PII redaction. These contexts could include specific keywords, phrases, or patterns that indicate sensitive information.

2. Modify the pipeline to include a custom script processor that analyzes the data for these contextual triggers. The script processor can be written using Painless, Elasticsearch's scripting language.

3. In the custom script processor, implement logic that checks the data for the identified contextual triggers. If a trigger is found, the script processor should modify the data to flag the relevant PII for redaction.

4. Update the NER and regex/grok pattern steps in the pipeline to redact PII only when it has been flagged by the custom script processor.

By implementing these expansion and enhancement options, you can create a customized PII redaction pipeline that is tailored to your organization's specific data and requirements. This ensures that your pipeline is both accurate and efficient, allowing you to effectively protect sensitive information while minimizing the risk of false positives or incomplete redactions.

One final, yet crucial, aspect to consider when implementing a PII redaction pipeline, or indeed any ingest pipeline, is the potential latency it may introduce to the data ingestion process. Each step incorporated into the ingest process inherently contributes to latency. However, the degree of this latency that can be deemed acceptable is largely a matter of individual or business discretion.

The user must understand the ramifications of several key points in this context. Firstly, it is imperative to measure the amount of latency the redaction pipeline introduces before the data becomes searchable. This is pivotal to maintain the balance between data protection and operational efficiency.

Secondly, the significance of redacting each type of data that the pipeline is configured for should be evaluated. This would involve a thorough understanding of the sensitivity of each data type and its potential impact on privacy and compliance concerns.

The third point revolves around determining the necessity of scanning every message, or whether sampling a subset would suffice. If the latter approach is chosen, the organization must then decide whether the non-sampled data containing PII needs to be sanitized and how easily it can be sanitized or deleted at a later time.

While detailed cluster benchmarking was covered in *Chapter 4, Performance Tuning—Working with Data*, some high-level approaches are worth mentioning here:

- Use Elasticsearch's Rally tool to compare ingesting data with and without the PII redaction pipeline.

> **Note**
> You should ensure some fake PII is in the logs to simulate the processing time for redacting information, not just scanning for data. See the section on Faker earlier in this chapter for an example of generating fake PII.

- Use a custom script or other performance tool you may already have set up.

- Use the `ingest_pipeline` metricset of the Elasticsearch module in Metricbeat to collect processor timing information. You can then monitor both testing data as well as ongoing and real-time production timing data of the processors and overall pipeline.

By keeping these considerations in mind while implementing a PII redaction pipeline, you can ensure that data privacy is upheld without compromising operational efficiency.

Summary

Throughout this chapter, we delved into the process of creating, configuring, and customizing a PII redaction pipeline in Elasticsearch, an essential tool for safeguarding sensitive information in today's data-driven world. You should now have a comprehensive understanding of how to set up the default pipeline, customize it according to your organization's unique requirements, and further enhance it by fine-tuning NER models or incorporating contextual awareness. Equipped with this knowledge, you are now well prepared to tackle the challenges of data privacy and security, ensuring that your organization complies with regulations and maintains the trust of its users by effectively protecting their personal information.

In the next chapter, we will explore how vector-search use cases can be combined with observability solutions in the Elastic platform.

7

Next Generation of Observability Powered by Vectors

As we move ahead in our journey to apply vectors to different use cases, we are going to see how to combine them with observability in this chapter. This domain is a part of the solution provided by the Elastic platform. Observability encompasses notions, such as log analytics, metric analytics, and **application performance monitoring** (**APM**), with the common purposes of building awareness about a system's health and helping operation teams to diagnose and remediate the root causes of incidents whenever they occur.

As systems become more complex, the management of these systems equally becomes complex for the operations teams. The data volumes generated by these systems keep increasing and become hard if not impossible for humans to follow, and in addition, are more and more volatile and distributed. One major aspect of any incident management workflow is interaction with data, whether through a query, a dashboard, or an alert. All these actions come down to one or more search queries. Every solution on the market has its own way of querying data, and in fact, companies rarely have a single solution for the multiple signals (logs, metrics, and more) they have to manage. They might even have separate solutions for metrics, logs, APM, and so on, which ultimately just adds even more complexity to the workflow.

With vectors, embeddings, and semantic search, there is a significant opportunity to reduce the aforementioned complexity by normalizing the query language—essentially by using NLP in any observability situation to interact with data. However, in order to be able to achieve this, operations teams need a platform versatile enough to provide the features of observability, traditional search, and semantic search. This is where Elastic has a significant advantage in the market, as it groups all of these essential features together.

In this chapter, we will focus on logs, as they are the most common element of observability. We will cover the following topics:

- The foundational concepts of observability

- Two approaches to providing semantic search functionality to operations teams for their logs

- The end-to-end implementation of this workflow using Elastic

Introduction to observability and its importance in modern software systems

Before getting into applying vectors to observability, it is important to take the time to understand the high-level concepts of observability itself.

Observability is the ability to understand the internal state of any layer that composes a system based on its external outputs. This was a relatively easy task when these systems were monoliths with multiple layers but produced a centralized log output that described the behavior of this "box." However, the process became more and more complicated as companies adopted decentralized cloud-native architectures such as microservices. The output for observability here becomes decorrelated, distributed, and composed of multiple signals, logs, metrics, and traces, to list but a few. Most vendors out there, including Elastic, have responded to this by striving to provide an integrated observability experience with the main goal of reducing **mean time to resolve** (**MTTR**) stats.

This space has seen rapid developments with a lot of actors getting involved and providing fantastic solutions to customers with the aim of facilitating the process of observing a software system.

Let's look into the signals that constitute the main pillars of observability.

Observability—main pillars

Signals are the data sources used to observe the health of an IT system. Signals report events, which can be broken down into structured and unstructured events (in the sense that some are very standard, such as Apache Logs, while others can be highly customized, such as logs coming from a custom Java application). In order for operations teams to observe their production runtime and understand what is happening, they need to be able to collect, aggregate, and correlate multiple signals and create alerts for them. Although new signals emerge as IT systems evolve, the basic, unavoidable signals are as follows:

- **Logs**: Logs are timestamped records of events that occur within the system. They are generated by infrastructure, applications, operating systems, network devices, and any number of other components in the system. They can carry a wide range of information spanning from simple status updates and user actions to errors and outages. Logs are often unstructured; indeed, the majority of logs are custom logs. Even in instances where these logs come from a somewhat standardized system (say, Apache servers), there is often a level of customization that makes them different from one deployment to another.

- **Metrics**: Metrics are numerical measurements that represent the state or performance of a system at a specific point in time. Common metrics include CPU usage, memory consumption, response time, storage capacity, error rates, and throughput. Metrics are systematic, often summarized, very structured, and are collected at regular intervals. The difference between metrics resides in the cardinality of the labels they carry. For example, in a Kubernetes cluster, which by itself is already complex despite its small size, the cardinality of metrics can increase with a lot of namespaces defined in the Kubernetes cluster.

- **Traces**: Traces involved in APM refer to a type of high-level signal that relates directly to a transaction taking place in a business application. To understand this better, consider logs as being phone calls you make that are displayed on your phone bill, while traces are the contents of the actual conversations. It is interesting to note that traces are a combination of logs and metrics. The complexity here resides in the ability to correlate different traces involved in the same overall transaction in a distributed decentralized system.

As you might have perceived by this point, it is by combining logs, metrics, and APM data that we can provide a comprehensive view of a system's state and behavior. Based on this, operations teams can receive notifications, investigate and diagnose issues, and identify the underlying causes of incidents.

Now, let's drill down into log analytics as we try to improve the log management process using vectors in this chapter.

Log analytics and its role in observability

The process of implementing log analytics for a given system has been around for decades and has morphed in different ways over time, but the crux of this process is still the same. The primary traditional approach to log analytics is for operations teams to connect to the problematic host, go through the log file, grep content, and hope for the best. While this process can work for very small deployments, it quickly becomes a headache when log volumes and the number of hosts grow. In light of this, solutions have been created to ship logs from different sources to a centralized place, parse them, and make them available for analytics.

Most solutions out there use the following process to do this:

1. An agent is deployed on a machine.
2. The agent sometimes applies some level of processing by enriching the log source or applying simple data transformations.
3. The agent ships the logs to a central server where additional processing takes place.
4. The user connects to a UI and starts searching, filtering, and aggregating logs with a query language and building dashboards.

Logs are not going anywhere; in fact, when we look at observability, even if the industry is trying to put signals into a specific category of their own, every signal is ultimately a form of log.

We believe the industry should focus on abstracting signals and proposing solutions that utilize the data and generate a user experience contextualized to the given persona… but that's for a different book. Although logs are the most popular and straightforward way to observe a system, there are various challenges associated with them, including the following:

- High volumes of logs require a scalable solution that offers decent performance when the end user analyzes them.

- As the log volume grows, the required infrastructure to support the observability platform goes up, which in turn leads to increased processing and storage costs.

- Log volumes can become overwhelming, and extracting the important information from all of the surrounding noise is not an easy process. Traditionally done manually, this process now benefits from the acceleration provided by machine learning techniques such as unsupervised learning and anomaly detection.

- Searching through logs and reducing response times requires structuring them. If logs are left unstructured, the search and analysis performance will be poor. However, the process of structuring logs can itself be overwhelming for non-technical users.

The challenges listed here all have specific solutions. We are going to focus on the operation team analyst experience, and more specifically, how to augment that experience with NLP.

A new approach—applying vectors and embeddings to log analytics

As you learned in *Chapter 1, Introduction to Vectors and Embeddings*, vectors and embeddings can be used to describe all sorts of notions and concepts, and we can build vector spaces that represent a given domain. When it comes to vectorizing logs, a couple of approaches are available. In the following sections, we will review two approaches that we believe are the most common ones: training or fine-tuning an existing model for logs and generating human-understandable descriptions and vectorizing these descriptions.

Approach 1—training or fine-tuning an existing model for logs

In this approach, an existing language model, such as *word2vec*, *BERT*, or *GPT*, is trained or fine-tuned specifically for log data. This means using a dataset of raw logs to adapt the model's parameters so that it can effectively capture the unique characteristics and patterns found in log data. The trained or fine-tuned model can then be used to vectorize raw logs, generating embeddings that represent the semantic content of the logs.

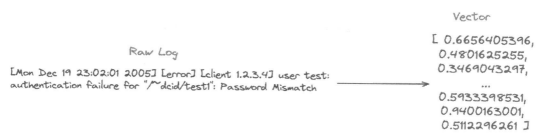

Figure 7.1: Log directly vectorized

Let's look at the pros and cons of this approach.

Pros

- **High accuracy**: When training or fine-tuning a model on logs, the model becomes specialized specifically to understand those logs and their structure. Therefore, the log embeddings generated by the models are much more accurate and closer to the true meaning of the given logs.

- **Direct vectorization**: With a specialized model, there won't be any intermediary processes. Raw logs are vectorized directly without the need for additional processing or human intervention, making the process more efficient and scalable.

- **Customization**: The model can be customized for specific types of logs (e.g., server logs or application logs) or specific log formats, which allows some level of flexibility based on the use case it is applied to.

Cons

- **Need for annotated data**: One of the main gaps in this approach is the training process itself. Training a model on logs requires a large representative dataset and, moreover, labeled data. This by itself is a high-calorie project; not impossible at all, just requiring a significant amount of work and constituting an expensive process.

- **Training complexity**: This is not to discourage you from this process, but note that training a dataset still remains a high hurdle in the machine learning space. It is computationally intensive, requires a specific set of skills, and lacks a democratized method.

- **Sensitivity to log format**: One of the major drawbacks of this approach is how volatile log structures can be, both from one source to another and in the same source across different deployments. The model will need to exhibit a certain level of resilience when facing log structure changes. This leads us back to our first con, which states that the dataset needs to be versatile enough for the model to be resilient.

Approach 2—generating human-understandable descriptions and vectorizing these descriptions

In this approach, a model is used to generate human-understandable descriptions of raw logs. These descriptions are then vectorized using a general-purpose language model (such as BERT or GPT) that has been trained on a large corpus of general text data. The resulting embeddings capture the semantic content of the descriptions derived from the original logs. We can see this process depicted in *Figure 7.2*.

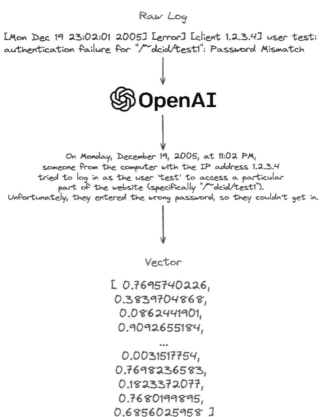

Figure 7.2: Log explained and then vectorized

Now, let's look at the pros and cons of this approach.

Pros

- **Interpretability**: By generating human-understandable descriptions, this approach provides a level of interpretability that can be useful for understanding and explaining the content of logs.

- **Flexibility**: This approach can be applied to different types of logs and log formats, as the model generates descriptions that are independent of the original log structure.

- **Utilization of pre-trained models**: Starting off with a pre-trained model that has been trained on a large corpus of text will save you time from training a model from scratch and give you immediate value. In some cases, you might lose accuracy, but you would still have the ability to fine-tune the model.

Cons

- **Loss of information**: You might lose some level of fidelity when generating descriptions from the original logs, especially if the descriptions are simplified or abstracted.

- **Additional processing**: The need to add a description can increase the overhead on the data collection pipeline, which can lead to poor performance. Therefore, we need to consider whether the log description generation process should be done when the log is stored or when it's read.

- **Quality of descriptions**: The quality of the embeddings depends on the quality of the generated descriptions. If the descriptions are not accurate or do not capture the key information from the logs, the embeddings may be less useful.

What's very interesting in this second approach is the fact that the logs are expanded and translated into a human-readable description. This allows us to avoid creating a specific vector space for the raw logs by training a model for it, as the expansion with OpenAI normalizes the logs to a version that can be vectorized. To summarize, vectorizing the expanded logs essentially allows us to transpose one vector space to the other without having to create the first one.

The other benefit here is that what was in the raw logs is now vectorized. These vectors are composed of meaningful embeddings that can easily be semantically correlated to other logs in the space.

In the next section, we will go through the process of expanding and vectorizing logs to get them ready for semantic search with vector search.

Log vectorization

Log vectorization is the process of transforming logs into embeddings. This process requires a couple of steps, such as generating logs for the test and expanding and using a general model to generate vectors.

In addition, we made the arbitrary choice to do everything in Python here, which gives you the ability to re-execute the same examples in a Google Colab notebook for educational purposes.

All the code from this chapter is available in the `chapter 7` folder of this book's GitHub repository: `https://github.com/PacktPublishing/Vector-Search-for-Practitioners-with-Elastic/tree/main/chapter7`.

Note that instead of applying the first approach and trying to generate vectors directly from the logs, we will adopt the strategy of expanding them to a human-readable description first, allowing us to avoid the intensive process of model training.

We are now going to learn how to generate synthetic logs.

Synthetic log

With synthetic logs, we enable users to test the entire pipeline without having to generate logs. Synthetic logs can be considered the same as the *mocks* used in any development project.

To be able to run the process for the purpose of testing in this book, we have prepared a block of code that will help generate synthetic logs. The following code blocks respectively generate Apache HTTP access logs, nginx, Syslog, AWS CloudTrail, Microsoft event logs, Linux audit logs, and more by heavily leveraging the `Faker` library.

Apache HTTP server (common log format)

The following code generates Apache HTTP Server log, we will see how to use the same code structure for all other log formats subsequently:

```
fake = Faker() #we use a single instance for the rest of the code
def generate_apache_log():
return
  '{RemoteHost} - - [{Timestamp}]
    "{RequestMethod}{RequestURI} {Protocol}" {StatusCode}
    {ResponseSize}'.format(RemoteHost=fake.ipv4(),
        Timestamp=fake.date_time_this_year()
            .strftime('%d/%b/%Y:%H:%M:%S %z'),
        RequestMethod=fake.http_method(),
        RequestURI=fake.uri(),
        Protocol='HTTP/1.1',
        StatusCode=random.choice([200, 404, 500]),
        ResponseSize=random.randint(100, 10000))
```

nginx (combined log format)

```
def generate_nginx_log():
return '{RemoteAddress} - {RemoteUser} [{Timestamp}] "{RequestMethod}
{RequestURI} {Protocol}" {StatusCode} {ResponseSize} "{Referer}"
"{UserAgent}"'.format(
RemoteAddress=fake.ipv4(),
RemoteUser='-',
Timestamp=fake.date_time_this_year().strftime('%d/%b/%Y:%H:%M:%S %z'),
RequestMethod=fake.http_method(),
```

```
RequestURI=fake.uri(),
Protocol='HTTP/1.1',
StatusCode=random.choice([200, 404, 500]),
ResponseSize=random.randint(100, 10000),
Referer=fake.uri(),
UserAgent=fake.user_agent()
)
```

Syslog (RFC 5424)

```
def generate_syslog():
return '<{Priority}>{Version} {Timestamp} {Hostname} {AppName}
{ProcID} {MsgID} {StructuredData} {Message}'.format(
Priority=random.randint(1, 191),
Version=1,
Timestamp=fake.date_time_this_year().isoformat(),
Hostname=fake.hostname(),
AppName=fake.word(),
ProcID=random.randint(1000, 9999),
MsgID=random.randint(1000, 9999),
StructuredData='-',
Message=fake.sentence()
)
```

AWS CloudTrail

```
def generate_aws_cloudtrail_log():
return '{{"eventVersion": "{EventVersion}", "userIdentity": {{"type":
"IAMUser", "userName": "{UserName}"}}, "eventTime": "{Timestamp}",
"eventSource": "{EventSource}", "eventName": "{EventName}",
"awsRegion": "{AwsRegion}", "sourceIPAddress": "{SourceIPAddress}",
"userAgent": "{UserAgent}", "requestParameters": {{"key":
"value"}}, "responseElements": {{"key": "value"}}, "requestID":
"{RequestId}", "eventID": "{EventId}", "eventType": "AwsApiCall",
"recipientAccountId": "{RecipientAccountId}"}}'.format(
EventVersion='1.08',
UserName=fake.user_name(),
Timestamp=fake.date_time_this_year().isoformat(),
EventSource='s3.amazonaws.com',
EventName='GetObject',
AwsRegion='us-east-1',
SourceIPAddress=fake.ipv4(),
UserAgent=fake.user_agent(),
RequestId=fake.uuid4(),
EventId=fake.uuid4(),
RecipientAccountId=fake.random_number(digits=12)
)
```

Microsoft Windows event log

```
def generate_windows_event_log():
return '<Event xmlns="http://schemas.microsoft.com/win/2004/08/events/
event"><System><Provider Name="{ProviderName}"/><EventID>{EventID}</
EventID><Level>{Level}</Level><TimeCreated
SystemTime="{Timestamp}"/><SourceName>{SourceName}</
SourceName><Computer>{Computer}</Computer></
System><EventData>{Message}</EventData></Event>'.format(
ProviderName=fake.word(),
EventID=random.randint(1000, 9999),
Level=random.randint(1, 5),
Timestamp=fake.date_time_this_year().isoformat(),
SourceName=fake.word(),
Computer=fake.hostname(),
Message=fake.sentence()
)
```

Linux audit log

```
def generate_linux_audit_log():
return 'type={AuditType} msg=audit({Timestamp}): {Message}'.format(
AuditType=fake.word(),
Timestamp=fake.date_time_this_year().isoformat(),
Message=fake.sentence()
)
```

Elasticsearch

```
def generate_elasticsearch_log():
return '{{"timestamp": "{Timestamp}", "level": "{LogLevel}",
"component": "{Component}", "cluster.name": "{ClusterName}", "node.
name": "{NodeName}", "message": "{Message}", "cluster.uuid":
"{ClusterUuid}", "node.id": "{NodeId}"}}'.format(
Timestamp=fake.date_time_this_year().isoformat(),
LogLevel=random.choice(['INFO', 'WARN', 'ERROR']),
Component=fake.word(),
ClusterName=fake.word(),
NodeName=fake.word(),
Message=fake.sentence(),
ClusterUuid=fake.uuid4(),
NodeId=fake.uuid4()
)
```

MySQL (general query log)

```
def generate_mysql_log():
return '{Timestamp} {ThreadID} {CommandType}          {CommandText}'.
format(
Timestamp=fake.date_time_this_year().isoformat(),
ThreadID=random.randint(1000, 9999),
CommandType=fake.word(),
CommandText=fake.sentence()
)
```

MongoDB (log format)

```
def generate_mongodb_log():
return '{Timestamp} {Severity} {Component} [{Context}] {Message}'.
format(
Timestamp=fake.date_time_this_year().isoformat(),
Severity=random.choice(['I', 'W', 'E']),
Component=fake.word(),
Context=fake.word(),
Message=fake.sentence()
)
```

Kafka (server log)

```
def generate_kafka_log():
return '[{Timestamp}] {LogLevel} {Component} ({ThreadName}) -
{Message}'.format(
Timestamp=fake.date_time_this_year().isoformat(),
LogLevel=random.choice(['INFO', 'WARN', 'ERROR']),
Component=fake.word(),
ThreadName=fake.word(),
Message=fake.sentence())
```

Now that we have our log generation infrastructure ready to simulate logs being sent by our applications, we are going to address log expansion.

Expanding logs at write with OpenAI

We now have a set of logs that are ready to be expanded. Here, the term "expanded" means that we are going to use the OpenAI model to explain the log, which consequently will expand it in size. The following code, present in the `chapter 7` folder of this book's GitHub repository, illustrates how to run the previous functions.

In this example, we have decided to generate Apache access logs:

```
# Example usage
sources_to_use = ['apache']
total_logs_to_generate = 15
random_logs_per_source = True
logs = generate_logs(sources_to_use, total_logs_to_generate, random_
logs_per_source)
stringifiedPromptsArray = json.dumps(logs)
prompts = [{
"role": "user",
"content": stringifiedPromptsArray
}]


batchInstruction = {
"role": "system",
    "content": "Explain what happened for each log line of the array.
Return a python array of the explanation. Only the array, no text
around it or any extra comment, nothing else than the array should be
in the answer. Don't forget in your completion to give the day, date
and year of the log. Interpret some of the log content if you can, for
example you have to translate what an error code 500 is."
}
prompts.append(batchInstruction)
# Define the OpenAI API key and Elasticsearch connection details
openai_api_key = "YOUR_OPEN_AI_KEY"

# Initialize the OpenAI API client
openai.api_key = openai_api_key
 stringifiedBatchCompletion = openai.ChatCompletion.create(model="gpt-
3.5-turbo",
messages=prompts,
max_tokens=1000)
print(stringifiedBatchCompletion.choices[0].message.content)
batchCompletion = ast.literal_eval(stringifiedBatchCompletion.
choices[0].message.content)
```

Notice that the prompt has been built by concatenating all the logs with a comma separator. This is because the OpenAI APIs don't provide the option to bulk a query. OpenAI will run prompts one at a time.

The input coming from the log generation function will look like this:

```
['200.19.87.161 - - [23/Mar/2023:23:03:39 ] "PATCH http://www.obrien-
arias.com/category/login.php HTTP/1.1" 200 9727', '202.90.114.96 - -
[11/Mar/2023:22:11:23 ] "CONNECT http://clark.com/terms/ HTTP/1.1"
200 7022', '198.55.207.252 - - [06/Apr/2023:05:43:19 ] "HEAD https://
```

```
www.ward.com/index.htm HTTP/1.1" 200 3016', '3.178.238.218 - - [21/
Jan/2023:12:08:38 ] "PUT http://www.hobbs.com/ HTTP/1.1" 500 8772',
'110.184.88.144 - - [09/Jan/2023:20:20:37 ] "DELETE https://robertson.
com/tag/author/ HTTP/1.1" 404 3548']
```

The expanded logs become the following:

```
["On March 23rd, 2023 at 11:03:39 PM, a PATCH HTTP request was sent
to http://www.obrien-arias.com/category/login.php and received a 200
response code with a payload size of 9727.",
"On March 11th, 2023 at 10:11:23 PM, a CONNECT HTTP request was sent
to http://clark.com/terms/ and received a 200 response code with a
payload size of 7022.",
"On April 6th, 2023 at 05:43:19 AM, a HEAD HTTP request was sent to
https://www.ward.com/index.htm and received a 200 response code with a
payload size of 3016.",
"On January 21st, 2023 at 12:08:38 PM, a PUT HTTP request was sent to
http://www.hobbs.com/ and received a 500 response code indicating an
internal server error, with a payload size of 8772.",
"On January 9th, 2023 at 08:20:37 PM, a DELETE HTTP request was sent
to https://robertson.com/tag/author/ and received a 404 response
indicating the page was not found, with a payload size of 3548."]
```

Expanding the logs makes it easier to find a general model to apply to the logs to vectorize them, which is what we are going to do in the next part.

Semantic search on our logs

In this section, we will focus on transforming the expanded logs into vectors in Elasticsearch and then implementing a semantic search functionality on top of the vectorized content. We do this because—remember—our logs are now stored in human-readable language, so we can apply to them the principles of NLP and semantic search we saw earlier.

Building a query using log vectorization

The following code takes the sequence of expanded logs to build a bulk indexing query for Elasticsearch:

```
# Generate the sequence of JSON documents for a bulk index operation
bulk_index_body = []
for index, log in enumerate(batchCompletion):
document = {
    "_index": "logs",
    "pipeline": "vectorize-log",
    "_source": {
            "text_field": log, "log": logs[index]
    }
}
bulk_index_body.append(document)
```

The code then executes the bulk indexing operation using a Python helper. Note that we do not apply vectorization in the Python code; instead, we have loaded a model in Elasticsearch using Eland:

```
try:
    response = helpers.bulk(es, bulk_index_body)
    print ("\nRESPONSE:", response)
except Exception as e:
    print("\nERROR:", e)
```

Loading a model

To learn more about loading models in Elasticsearch, I recommend you read this blog post from Jeff on the Elastic website: `https://www.elastic.co/blog/chatgpt-elasticsearch-openai-meets-private-data`.

Also see the following link demonstrating an example of loading a model using Eland: `https://github.com/jeffvestal/ElasticDocs_GPT/blob/main/load_embedding_model.ipynb`.

The example shows how you can download a model from Hugging Face and load it into Elasticsearch using a couple of lines of Python code:

```
# Set the model name from Hugging Face and task type hf_model_
id='sentence-transformers/all-distilroberta-v1'
tm = TransformerModel(hf_model_id, "text_embedding")

#set the modelID as it is named in Elasticsearch es_model_id =
tm.elasticsearch_model_id()

# Download the model from Hugging Face
tmp_path = "models"
Path(tmp_path).mkdir(parents=True, exist_ok=True) model_path, config,
vocab_path = tm.save(tmp_path)

# Load the model into Elasticsearch ptm = PyTorchModel(es, es_model_
id) ptm.import_model(model_path=model_path, config_path=None, vocab_
path=vocab_path, config=config)
```

Ultimately, in **Kibana** | **Machine Learning** | **Model Management** | **Trained Models**, you should see the model has been loaded:

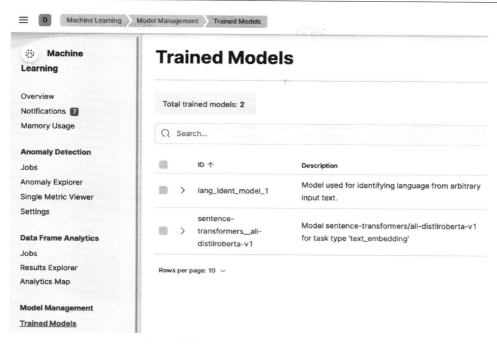

Figure 7.3: Loaded trained model in Kibana

Ingest pipeline

Now, you might have noticed in the previous bulk indexing code that we reference a pipeline called `vectorize-log`. This pipeline is intended to use the model that we loaded to generate vectors from the expanded logs. To define a pipeline, you can go to **Kibana | Stack Management | Ingest Pipelines** or try my preferred technique, which is to push a pipeline via the create pipeline API (`https://www.elastic.co/guide/en/elasticsearch/reference/current/put-pipeline-api.html`).

Here is the definition of our pipeline:

```
[
  {
    "inference": {
      "model_id": "sentence-transformers__all-distilroberta-v1",
      "target_field": "description_vectorized"
    }
  },
  {
    "set": {
      "field": "description_vectorized",
```

```
        "copy_from": "description_vectorized.predicted_value"
    }
  },
  {
    "grok": {
      "field": "log",
      "patterns": [
        "%{IP:source.ip} - - \\[%{DATE_YMD:@timestamp}\\]
\"%{WORD:http.request.method} %{DATA:url.original} HTTP/%{NUMBER:http.
version}\" %{NUMBER:http.response.status_code:int}"
      ],
      "pattern_definitions": {
        "DATE_YMD":
"%{MONTHDAY}/%{MONTH}/%{YEAR}%{SPACE}%{HOUR}:%{MINUTE}: \
?%{SECOND}%{SPACE}"
      }
    }
  }
]
```

Each JSON object in this JSON array is a processor. We have three of them in total:

- **Inference**: The first one references the ID of the model we loaded. This is done to vectorize the content of the field with the name `text_field` to a field called `description_vectorized`.

- **Set**: The second processor is used to format the output JSON. You will see that if you don't have this processor, the `description_vectorized` output field will have a subfield called `predicted_value` in which the vector is stored, but that's not what we want. Our aim is to store the vector directly in our `description_vectorized` dense vector field without any unnecessary subfields being introduced.

- **Grok**: Lastly, with the Grok processor, we parse the log to be more structured. The eventual goal here is to use the structured log for aggregation and analytics.

By this point, you now have a grasp on how to model your data in a way that enables you to keep the source log, benefit from a structured data model, and have vectorized content with which you can initiate a semantic search.

Semantic search

We are now going to build a function that calls the kNN API to do two things:

- Make a query to filter documents for those where the `description_vectorized` field exists

- Run the actual vector search

Here is the ESSearch function implementation:

```
def ESSearch(query_text):
# Elasticsearch query (BM25) and kNN configuration for hybrid search
query = {
"bool": {
        "filter": [{
            "exists": {
                "field": "description_vectorized"
            }
}]
}
}

knn = {
    "field": "description_vectorized",
    "k": 1,
    "num_candidates": 20,
    "query_vector_builder": {
        "text_embedding": {
            "model_id": "sentence-transformers__all-distilroberta-v1",
            "model_text": query_text
        }
    },
    "boost": 24
}

fields = ["text_field"]
index = 'logs'
resp = es.search(index=index, query=query, knn=knn, fields=fields,
size=1, source=False)
print(resp['hits']['hits'][0]['fields']['text_field'][0])
return resp['hits']['hits'][0]['fields']['text_field'][0]
```

An interesting aspect of this code is the use of the semantic search feature (https://www.elastic.co/guide/en/elasticsearch/reference/master/knn-search.html#semantic-search), which essentially spares the user from vectorizing the query and passing the vector as an argument to the kNN search. The semantic search query allows users to directly pass the text version of the query and the model that has been used to vectorize the indexed document. As a result, the query and the document are vectorized in the same vector space.

To use the function, simply call the function with the query you want to submit to Elastic:

```
ESSearch("Were there any errors?")
```

The result should look like this:

```
On March 8th, 2023 at 09:27:46 AM, a GET HTTP request was sent to
https://www.pratt.com/faq.htm and received a 404 response indicating
the page was not found, with a payload size of 3510.
```

The simplicity of a semantic search implementation with Elasticsearch is so disconcerting that we forget the significant value it delivers for **site reliability engineering** (**SRE**) in terms of our understanding of what's happening in our system based on our logs. Operations teams can simply query the system with natural language and get the most relevant pieces of information to guide them through their investigation.

The expansion of logs is a substantial improvement in the incident management process, taking all the complexity of log management away from the operations team, who no longer need to learn a specific language for the given observability solution to interact with their data. Instead, operations teams can now come up with their own language.

The learning curve is thus significantly reduced, not only for querying data but also for automation, as the same semantic search queries can be used to define alerts. This can also be taken further, with the results of the alerts expanded into a ticket with a recommended solution. There is a lot of potential in leveraging vectors to automate manual effort in our current workflows, reducing the MTTR and increasing our application's users' satisfaction.

Summary

In this chapter, you hopefully have learned the end-to-end process of setting up log vectorization for your log analysis workload based on Elastic. One important point for you to decide on while doing this is whether you expand the log on write or on read, meaning preparing the data while ingesting it or expanding to the meaning of the raw log only when querying it. As you can appreciate, this is still an exploratory domain where applying vector search, or GenAI, to accelerate observability incident management workflow is just beginning to murmur. But you are now prepared with the necessary guidance to implement it as it grows.

In the next chapter, we will address another domain of application for vectors and semantic search—cybersecurity, where the requirements are pretty similar to observability in terms of data, but the workflow is quite different.

8

The Power of Vectors and Embedding in Bolstering Cybersecurity

In the face of ever-evolving cybersecurity threats, a constant influx of information demands innovative tools and methods for sifting through vast datasets. The challenge becomes particularly daunting when determining the nuances and intentions behind the text.

For instance, as phishing attacks are becoming increasingly sophisticated, how can we identify what is malicious from what is benign, especially when they seem so alike? Enter **Elastic Learned Sparse EncodeR** (**ELSER**): a potent tool designed to understand text at a semantic level and discern the patterns and intents underneath the surface.

This chapter dives deep into ELSER, a pre-trained model provided by Elastic that has harnessed the power of vectors without burdening the user with its intricacies. We will address the following key topics:

- Overview of ELSER, where we will delve into its essence and role in semantic search

- Handling data with ELSER, including the steps for uploading, visualizing, and processing data

- Utilizing ELSER to identify potential phishing threats

By the end of this chapter, you will not only have grasped the vast potential of ELSER but will also be equipped to integrate it into various applications beyond just cybersecurity.

Technical requirements

In this chapter, you are going to set up your Elastic environment to use ELSER. For this, you will need to create an Elastic Cloud account at `https://cloud.elastic.co/registration`.

ELSER is a commercial feature under the platinum license. The good news is that Elastic provides a trial period to test it. Throughout your trial, you will be able to ask the Customer Engineers team questions through the chatbot, and they'll guide you through the experience.

Understanding the importance of email phishing detection

Before getting into ELSER and its application in cybersecurity, we will understand phishing thoroughly and then move on to more advanced techniques with semantic search.

What is phishing?

Phishing is a common type of cyber-attack that involves disguising oneself as a reliable entity in electronic communication to gain sensitive information such as credentials, such as usernames and passwords, and payment information such as credit card or social security numbers.

Email spoofing is the main method used to phish. With the increase in communication apps, phishing also happens on platforms that offer instant messaging and often directs users to enter personal information on a fake website that matches the look and feel of a legitimate site.

Phishing directly affects thousands of people each day. Cybercriminals use social engineering techniques to trick unsuspecting individuals and organizations into giving up sensitive information or making transactions to accounts controlled by criminals.

The term "phishing" is a play on the word "*fishing*," as these scams involve baiting victims and reeling them in, much like the sport of fishing. The "*ph*" is a common hacker replacement for "*f*" and is a nod to the original form of hacking, known as "*phreaking*."

Phishing attacks can range from simple and generic to highly sophisticated and targeted. The most dangerous types, such as spear phishing and whaling, specifically target individuals or organizations and are meticulously planned to yield high returns for the attackers.

We recommend you go through Wikipedia's extensive content on phishing: `https://en.wikipedia.org/wiki/Phishing`.

Now, let's look at the different types of phishing.

Different types of phishing attacks

Let's look at the different forms of phishing depending on the context or the persona it targets:

- **Spear phishing**: This is a targeted form of phishing where the attacker has done their homework. They personalize their emails with the target's name, position, company, work phone number, and other information to make the email seem less suspicious. The goal is to trick the recipient into believing that they have a connection to the attacker.

- **Whaling**: This is a form of phishing attack that targets high-profile employees, such as CEOs or CFOs, to steal sensitive information from a company, as these individuals often have total access to sensitive company data.

- **Clone phishing**: This type of phishing attack involves taking a previously delivered email with its content and recipient address(es) and creating an almost identical or cloned email. The original attachment or link in the email is replaced with a malicious version and then sent from an email address spoofed to appear to come from the original sender.

- **Pharming**: Pharming is a more complex method of phishing that involves malicious code and fraudulent websites. The attacker installs malicious code on the user's computer or server that redirects clicks made by a user in their web browser to a fraudulent website without their consent or knowledge.

- **Smishing and vishing**: These terms are used to describe phishing attacks that take place over SMS text messages (**smishing**) and voice calls (**vishing**).

- **Business Email Compromise** (**BEC**): This is a sophisticated scam that targets businesses working with foreign suppliers and/or businesses that regularly perform wire transfer payments. The scam is carried out by compromising legitimate business email accounts through social engineering or computer intrusion techniques to conduct unauthorized transfers of funds.

Each of these types of phishing attacks has its unique characteristics, but they all share the same goal: to trick the victim into revealing sensitive information.

While phishing can be carried out in different ways, this chapter will specifically focus on email phishing, which is one of the most common and pervasive vehicles for phishing attacks.

Email phishing is a significant threat because of its ability to reach a vast number of potential victims at once. It's a method favored by many cybercriminals due to its simplicity and effectiveness. Attackers can send out thousands of fraudulent emails with the click of a button, and all it takes is one unsuspecting recipient to take the bait for the attack to be successful.

We will explore how they are structured, why they are effective, and most importantly, how we can use tools such as ELSER from Elastic to detect and prevent them. We will use a real-world dataset of emails, labeled as **ham** (legitimate) or **spam** (phishing), to demonstrate how these tools can be applied in practice.

By focusing on email phishing, we aim to provide you with a deep understanding of this specific threat and equip you with the knowledge and tools to combat it effectively. This focus is particularly relevant given the increasing reliance on digital communication in both personal and professional settings, which has been accompanied by a rise in email phishing attempts.

Statistics on the frequency of phishing attacks

Before diving into the technical considerations, I thought it would be important for us to understand the challenges phishing creates in our society and their impact. Of course, there will always be ways for attackers to innovate their approach to phishing. However, there are strong defenses that companies can deploy, including more intelligent detection based on text semantics, which will help minimize the challenge. Here are some global statistics on the frequency of phishing attacks:

- There are an estimated 3.4 billion phishing emails sent every single day
- About 90% of data breaches occur due to phishing
- 83% of organizations have experienced a phishing attack in the past year
- The average cost of dealing with a phishing attack is $1.8 million
- The most common phishing scam strategies are as follows:

  - Emails that appear to be from a legitimate company, such as your bank or credit card company. These emails often ask you to click on a link or provide personal information, such as your password or credit card number.
  - Emails that contain attachments that are infected with malware. When you open these attachments, the malware can infect your computer and steal your personal information.
  - Text messages that appear to be from a legitimate company, such as your shipping company. These text messages often ask you to click on a link or provide personal information, such as your tracking number.

Here are a couple of notable examples of phishing attacks and their impact:

- **The Facebook and Google scam**: In 2013, a spear phishing scam was sent to millions of Facebook users. The email appeared to be from Facebook and asked users to click on a link to update their account information. When users clicked on the link, they were taken to a fake Facebook website that was designed to steal their login credentials.
- **The NotPetya malware attack**: In 2017, a clone phishing attack was used to deliver the *NotPetya* malware. The malware was disguised as an invoice from a shipping company and was sent to employees at several large companies, including Maersk and FedEx. When employees opened the attachment, the malware infected their computers and spread to other computers on the network. The attack caused billions of dollars in damage.

- **The Ukrainian power grid attack**: In 2015, a spear phishing attack was used to gain access to the Ukrainian power grid. The attack was carried out by a group of hackers known as *Sandworm*. The hackers used phishing emails to trick employees into clicking on links that infected their computers with malware. The malware gave the hackers control of the power grid and allowed them to shut down power in parts of Ukraine.

- **The Ubiquity Networks social engineering attack**: In 2018, a social engineering attack was used to steal data from Ubiquity Networks, an organization that sells wireless and wired products for homes and businesses. The spear phishing attack was carried out by a group of hackers known as *Cobalt Strike*. The hackers posed as a legitimate company and sent phishing emails to employees at Ubiquity Networks. The emails contained links that infected the employees' computers with malware. The malware gave the hackers access to the company's network and allowed them to steal data.

- **The FACC BEC attack**: In 2019, a whaling/BEC attack was used to steal $100 million from FACC. The attack was carried out by a group of hackers who impersonated FACC's CEO in a series of emails. The emails instructed employees to wire money to a fraudulent bank account. The employees complied with the instructions and the hackers were able to steal the money.

The impacts of email phishing span financial losses, data breaches, reputational damage, disruption of operations, and legal and regulatory consequences.

Now that we know the various types of phishing and some real attacks, let's analyze the challenges in detecting phishing emails.

Challenges in detecting phishing emails

Detecting phishing emails is akin to finding a needle in a haystack, and it's a task that has become increasingly difficult due to the sophistication of modern attacks.

For instance, a phishing email might perfectly replicate the branding, style, and tone of an email from a well-known bank. It might even appear to come from an official email address, thanks to techniques such as email spoofing. The email might contain a link to a website that is a near-perfect copy of the bank's official site, tricking the recipient into entering their login details.

Moreover, the challenge of detecting phishing emails is not just about technology; it's also about human nature. Even the most advanced email filtering system can't fully protect against human error. People are naturally inclined to trust and respond to urgent requests, especially when they appear to come from authoritative sources. A well-crafted phishing email can exploit these tendencies, tricking even the most vigilant individuals into clicking a malicious link or downloading an infected attachment.

For example, an employee might receive an email that appears to come from their company's IT department, urging them to update their password immediately due to a suspected security breach. Concerned about protecting their account, the employee clicks the link in the email, unknowingly falling into the phisher's trap.

These challenges underscore the need for advanced detection methods that can keep up with the evolving tactics of cybercriminals, as well as ongoing education to help individuals recognize and avoid phishing attempts.

Let's take a look at traditional automated detection—how it captures events that appear to be phishing attacks and its limits.

Role of automated detection

In the face of the challenges posed by phishing, automated detection plays a crucial role, much like a vigilant guard dog that never sleeps, constantly monitoring for signs of intrusion.

Traditional security measures, such as firewalls and antivirus software, are essential, but they're not always enough to catch phishing emails. These methods often rely on detecting known threats, such as specific malware signatures. However, phishing emails can slip through these defenses by using social engineering techniques rather than known malware. It's like trying to catch a chameleon: the threat is constantly changing its appearance to blend in with its surroundings.

That's where automated detection comes in. By using advanced techniques such as machine learning and natural language processing, automated systems can analyze the content and context of emails to detect signs of phishing. They can look for subtle clues that might be invisible to the human eye, such as slight discrepancies in email addresses or unusual patterns in the email's text.

For instance, an automated system might notice that an email claiming to be from a major bank is actually from an email address that's slightly different from the bank's official email address, or it might detect that the language in the email is unusually urgent or threatening, which is a common tactic in phishing emails.

Moreover, automated systems can process vast amounts of data at high speed, allowing them to catch phishing emails before they reach the recipient's inbox.

However, it's important to note that no system is perfect. Automated detection can significantly reduce the risk of phishing, but it can't eliminate it entirely. That's why it's crucial to combine automated detection with user education, to ensure that individuals know how to recognize and respond to any phishing attempts that do slip through the net.

The content of the email, its semantics, and the intent behind it are all critical aspects of a phishing attack. In fact, it's often the manipulation of these elements that makes phishing attacks so deceptive and effective.

Imagine a phishing email as a wolf in sheep's clothing. The wolf isn't just wearing the sheep's wool; it's also learned to behave like a sheep and bleat like a sheep. It mimics the behavior and communication of the sheep to blend in. Similarly, a phishing email doesn't just look like a legitimate email; it also tries to sound like one. It uses language, tone, and content that mimic the legitimate emails the recipient is used to receiving.

This is where the power of semantic understanding comes into play. By understanding the semantics of an email, an automated detection system can analyze not just the superficial characteristics of the email but also its underlying intent. It can recognize when an email that looks like a routine password update request is actually a phishing attempt. It can detect when an email that appears to be from a colleague is actually a cleverly disguised attack.

This is why technologies such as ELSER from Elastic, which are designed to understand the semantics of text, are so valuable in the fight against phishing. By understanding the content and intent of emails, these systems can enhance detection capabilities and provide a stronger defense against phishing attacks.

Augmenting existing techniques with natural language processing

As we navigate this complex terrain, our next guidepost is an exploration of ELSER, a pre-trained model developed by Elastic that brings together the power of embeddings and semantic understanding to bear the problem of phishing detection. In the upcoming section, we will delve into what ELSER is, how it works, and most importantly, how it can be harnessed to enhance our ability to detect and thwart phishing attacks. By understanding the semantics of text, ELSER offers a new way to see through the disguises of phishing emails, providing a stronger, more nuanced defense against this pervasive threat. So, let's embark on this journey of discovery, and see how ELSER can empower us in the fight against email phishing.

Introducing ELSER

ELSER is a groundbreaking tool that brings the power of machine learning to semantic search. It's capable of discerning the underlying meaning and intent of the text. This is particularly valuable in tasks such as email phishing detection, where understanding the content of an email is crucial for identifying threats.

Imagine trying to understand a corpus of text. Traditional methods might involve painstakingly analyzing each sentence, looking up unfamiliar words, and trying to piece together the overall meaning. This can be a slow and laborious process. ELSER, on the other hand, can instantly provide a detailed analysis of the text, highlighting the key themes and explaining the subtle nuances. What ELSER does uniquely is perform text expansion, creating a set of tokens that form a semantic space, allowing for a richer understanding of any text field it processes.

One of the standout features of ELSER is its user-friendly nature. ELSER offers an out-of-the-box solution where the user can push data into Elasticsearch and immediately benefit from semantic search capabilities, which significantly reduces the time to value. However, ELSER isn't just about speed; it's also about flexibility and scalability. As part of the Elastic platform, it can easily scale to handle large volumes of data, making it suitable for everything from small projects to enterprise-level applications. It's like a high-performance sports car that can effortlessly switch between cruising city streets and racing on a professional track.

However, it's important to note that ELSER is currently in technical preview, meaning it's still being refined and improved. Nevertheless, even in its current state, ELSER represents a significant step forward in semantic search.

In the upcoming sections, we'll delve deeper into how ELSER can be applied to the task of email phishing detection. We'll see how this innovative tool, with its combination of speed, flexibility, and power, can enhance cybersecurity efforts and provide a robust defense against phishing attacks.

The role of ELSER in GenAI

ELSER is not just a tool in isolation; it's part of a broader movement in the tech industry toward democratizing advanced technologies such as vector search, **large language models** (**LLMs**), and **generative artificial intelligence** (**GenAI**). It's a bit like the advent of personal computers in the 1980s, which brought computing power into the hands of everyday users, sparking a revolution in how we work, communicate, and entertain ourselves.

Tools such as ELSER are making advanced AI capabilities accessible to a wider range of users. Vector search, which involves converting text into high-dimensional vectors and searching for similar vectors, was once a complex process that required specialized knowledge and resources. Now, with ELSER, users can leverage the power of vector search without needing to understand the underlying complexities.

LLMs such as GPT have made headlines with their ability to generate human-like text, but their use has been largely confined to researchers and large tech companies. Tools such as ELSER are helping to democratize these models, making their capabilities available to a wider range of users.

This democratization is part of the GenAI movement, which aims to make GenAI accessible to and beneficial for all. By bringing advanced AI capabilities to the masses, tools such as ELSER are helping to drive this revolution, breaking down barriers and opening up new possibilities for individuals and businesses alike. As we explore how ELSER can be applied to email phishing detection, we'll see how this democratization of AI can have real-world impacts, enhancing cybersecurity and helping to protect against threats.

In our exploration of ELSER, we saw how this innovative tool harnesses the power of ML to bring a new level of understanding to semantic search. Like a master linguist, ELSER interprets the nuanced language of data, encoding the first few hundred words of a document to provide automatic semantic enrichments. Despite its current limitations, such as focusing on English text and considering only the first part of a document, ELSER represents a significant advancement in the field of text analysis. It's like having a high-powered microscope that allows us to see the intricate details of text, enhancing our ability to detect patterns, understand intent, and ultimately, identify threats such as phishing emails.

As we move forward, we'll apply these insights to a real-world challenge: email phishing detection. In the next section, we'll introduce the dataset we'll be using for this task—the Enron email dataset, which has been labeled as ham (legitimate) or spam (phishing). This dataset will serve as our testing ground, allowing us to see ELSER in action and explore how its semantic understanding capabilities can enhance our ability to detect phishing emails. So, let's dive in and see what insights this dataset holds.

Introduction to the Enron email dataset (ham or spam)

The Enron dataset is a large collection of email data that has become a staple in the world of text analysis and machine learning. It's like a vast library, filled with a diverse range of texts that offers a wealth of insights for those who know how to interpret them.

This dataset was originally made public during the legal investigation into Enron Corporation, a US energy company that collapsed in 2001 due to widespread corporate fraud. The dataset contains over 600,000 emails from about 150 users, mostly senior management of Enron, making it one of the only publicly available collections of real emails of its size.

For our purposes, the emails contained in the Enron dataset have been labeled as ham (legitimate) or spam (phishing). This labeling provides a valuable ground truth, allowing us to train and test models for phishing detection. Labeling tells us which emails are safe and which are dangerous, helping us to understand the characteristics of phishing emails and improve our detection methods.

However, it's important to note that the Enron dataset, like any dataset, has its limitations. The emails in the dataset are from the early 2000s and reflect the communication styles and security threats of that time. While many of the principles of phishing remain the same, the specific tactics and techniques used by phishers have evolved over time. Therefore, while the Enron dataset provides a valuable resource and example for our book for understanding and detecting phishing emails, it's important to complement this data with more recent examples and ongoing learning.

In this book, we are going to use the version of the Enron dataset hosted in the following GitHub repository: `https://github.com/MWiechmann/enron_spam_data`.

The Enron dataset we'll be working with is structured as a CSV file, where each row represents an email, and each column represents a specific attribute of that email.

The dataset consists of five columns:

- `Message ID`: This is a unique identifier for each email, much like a serial number. It helps us keep track of individual emails and reference them as needed.

- `Subject`: This is the subject line of the email. It's like the title of a book, providing a brief overview of the email's content.

- `Message`: This is the body of the email. It's the main content, where the sender communicates their message to the recipient.

- `Spam/Ham`: This is the label assigned to each email, indicating whether it's spam (a phishing email) or ham (a legitimate email). It's like a traffic light, signaling whether an email is safe (green) or potentially dangerous (red).

- `Date`: This is the date the email was sent. It provides a temporal context for each email, helping us understand when the communication occurred.

Here's an example of a message in CSV:

```
Message ID: 3675
Subject: await your response
Message: " dear partner , we are a team of government officials (...)
john adams ( chairman senate committee on banks and currency ) call
number : 234 - 802 - 306 - 8507"
Spam/Ham: spam
Date: 2003-12-18
```

This email is labeled as spam, indicating that it's a phishing email. The subject and message provide the content of the email, while the date tells us when it was sent. `Message ID` allows us to uniquely identify this email within the dataset.

In the upcoming sections, we'll explore how to use this dataset in conjunction with ELSER to enhance our ability to detect phishing emails.

Another way to look at this is to load the dataset in Elasticsearch and use the data visualizer in Kibana. To do this, first, connect to your Kibana instance and go to the **Machine Learning | Data Visualizer | File** section:

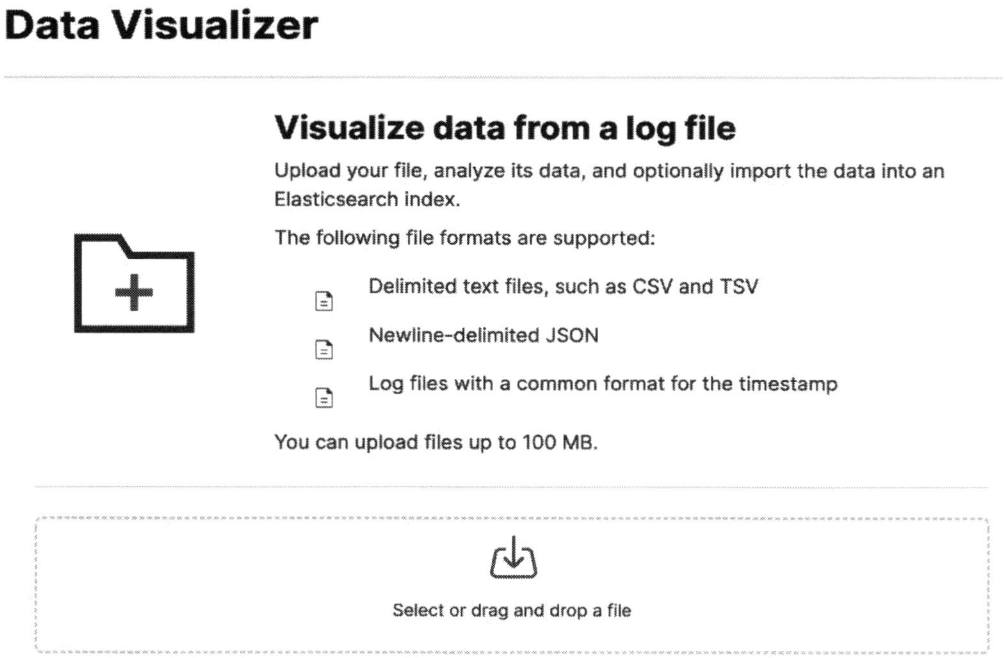

Data Visualizer

Visualize data from a log file

Upload your file, analyze its data, and optionally import the data into an Elasticsearch index.

The following file formats are supported:

- Delimited text files, such as CSV and TSV
- Newline-delimited JSON
- Log files with a common format for the timestamp

You can upload files up to 100 MB.

Select or drag and drop a file

Figure 8.1: File view in Kibana

From there, go ahead and upload the `enron_spam_data.csv` file; you should get the following summary before importing the file:

Data Visualizer

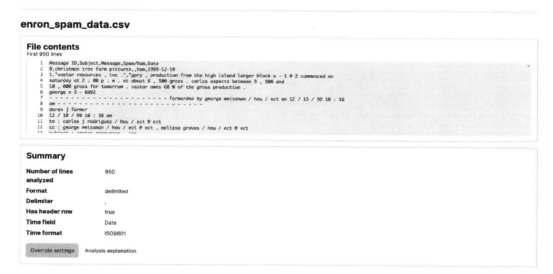

enron_spam_data.csv

File contents
First 950 lines

```
 1   Message ID,Subject,Message,Spam/Ham,Date
 2   0,christmas tree farm pictures,,ham,1999-12-10
 3   1,"vastar resources , inc .","gary , production from the high island larger block a - 1 # 2 commenced on
 4   saturday at 2 : 00 p . m . at about 6 , 500 gross . carlos expects between 9 , 500 and
 5   10 , 000 gross for tomorrow . vastar owns 68 % of the gross production .
 6   george x 3 - 6992
 7   - - - - - - - - - - - - - - - - - - - - - - - - - forwarded by george weissman / hou / ect on 12 / 13 / 99 10 : 16
 8   am - - - - - - - - - - - - - - - - - - - - - - - - - - -
 9   daren j farmer
10   12 / 10 / 99 10 : 38 am
11   to : carlos j rodriguez / hou / ect @ ect
12   cc : george weissman / hou / ect @ ect , melissa graves / hou / ect @ ect
13   subject : vastar resources , inc .
```

Summary

Number of lines analyzed	950
Format	delimited
Delimiter	,
Has header row	true
Time field	Date
Time format	ISO8601

Override settings   Analysis explanation

Figure 8.2: File upload summary

The data visualizer takes a sample: in this case, the first 950 first lines. Click on the **Import** button, set **Index name**, and confirm import:

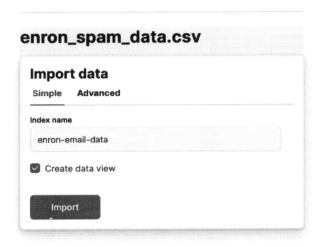

Figure 8.3: Index name

You should see the following confirmation screen:

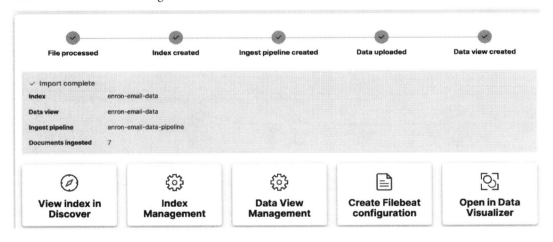

Figure 8.4: File upload confirmation screen

Click on the **Open in Data Visualizer** button to display the following chart:

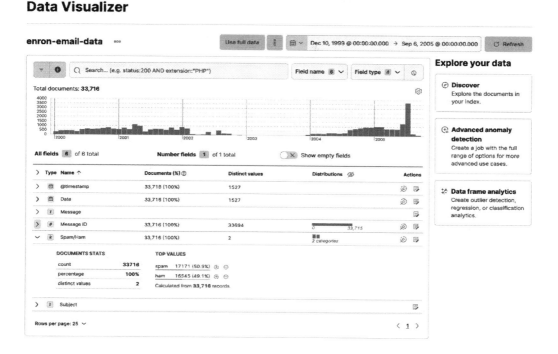

Figure 8.5: Data distribution

We can see that the index contains more than 33,000 emails, with 2 labels—spam and ham—where just over half of the emails are spam and the rest are ham. We are lucky to have such a straightforward dataset and reference to use with ELSER, as the heavy lifting has already been done for us from a data structuring perspective, and the data import functionality allows us to quickly onboard the data in Elastic. Next, we are going to see ELSER in action on top of this data and start detecting spam inside the dataset to verify whether we land close to the labeling that has been prepared already.

Seeing ELSER in action

In this part, we are going to walk you through how easy it is to get started with ELSER and see some significant results right out of the box. The first part will be to go through the required hardware. Then, we will look at preparing the index; finally, we are going to fire a couple of queries to illustrate the power of ELSER.

Hardware consideration

The ELSER documentation (`https://www.elastic.co/guide/en/machine-learning/current/ml-nlp-elser.html#elser-hw-benchamrks`) goes through benchmarks in representative data, which highlights KPIs such as inference, indexing, query, and latency.

You will see there that the hardware configuration significantly impacts the performance of ELSER. Here are some key takeaways to consider for sizing your infrastructure:

- **CPU and memory**: The more powerful the ML node (in terms of CPU and memory), the better the performance. For instance, an ML node with 16 GB of memory and 8 vCPUs performs better than one with 4 GB of memory and 2 vCPUs. This is evident in terms of both inference times and indexing speed.

- **Thread allocation**: The way threads are allocated also matters. For example, a single allocation with multiple threads (8, in this case) on a 16-GB, 8-vCPU ML node significantly improves inference times and reduces the query latency compared to multiple allocations with a single thread each.

- **Dataset characteristics**: The characteristics of the dataset, such as the length of documents and queries, can impact performance. Longer documents and queries may increase inference times and query latency.

To sum up, for optimal ELSER performance, the results suggest using a powerful ML node (high memory and CPU) and allocating multiple threads to a single allocation. This will increase the pace at which a single inference is processed by multiple threads. However, these are general guidelines, so the recommendation is always to test for your dataset and available hardware.

Downloading the ELSER model in Elastic

By default, the model isn't deployed in Elastic. You will need to go to **Machine Learning | Trained Models** in Kibana, click on the **Download** button next to the ELSER model in the list, and start the model so that you see the following:

Start .elser_model_1 deployment   ×

ⓘ The product of the number of allocations and threads per allocation should be less than the total number of processors on your ML nodes.

Deployment ID
Specify unique identifier for the model deployment.

Deployment ID

.elser_model_1

Priority
Select low priority for demonstrations where each model
will be very lightly used.

Priority

| low | normal |

Number of allocations
Increase to improve throughput of all requests.

Number of allocations

1

Threads per allocation
Increase to improve latency for each request.

Threads per allocation

| 1 | 2 | 4 | 8 |

Learn more ☒   Cancel   Start

Figure 8.6: Starting ELSER

In the preceding screenshot, we set the deployment name to `.elser_model_1` and start the model.
You should now have a running ELSER model as follows:

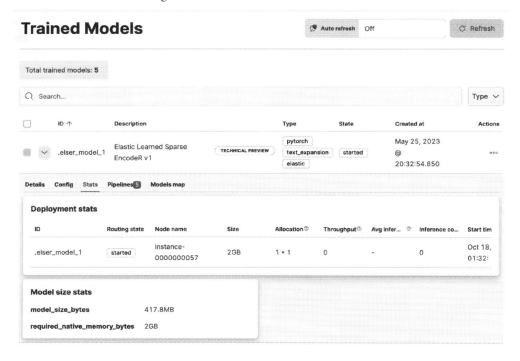

Figure 8.7: ELSER downloaded and deployed

We are now going to see how to create an index and reindex our data in order to use ELSER.

Setting up the index and ingestion pipeline

ELSER expands the text contained in your dataset into meaningful tokens that are part of the same semantic space. In this regard, the destination index needs to be mapped with a field of the rank_ features type.

You can find more documentation about the rank features at the following link: https://www. elastic.co/guide/en/elasticsearch/reference/current/rank-features. html.

Index mapping

In our example, we are going to create an index called enron-email-data-elsered with the same mapping as the previous index but with an additional field to store the tokens generated by ELSER. To get the current index mapping, run the following API call in **Kibana | Dev Tools**:

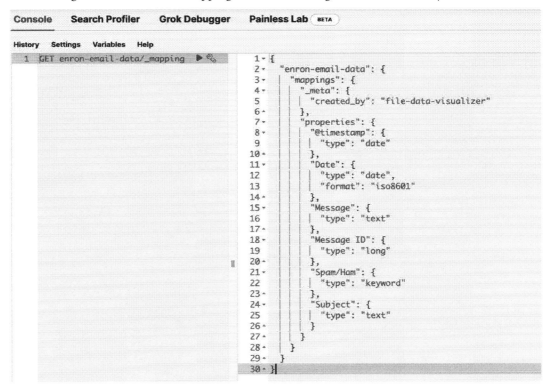

Figure 8.8: Raw data mapping

Still in **Kibana | Dev Tools**, we are now going to create a new mapping and add our new field:

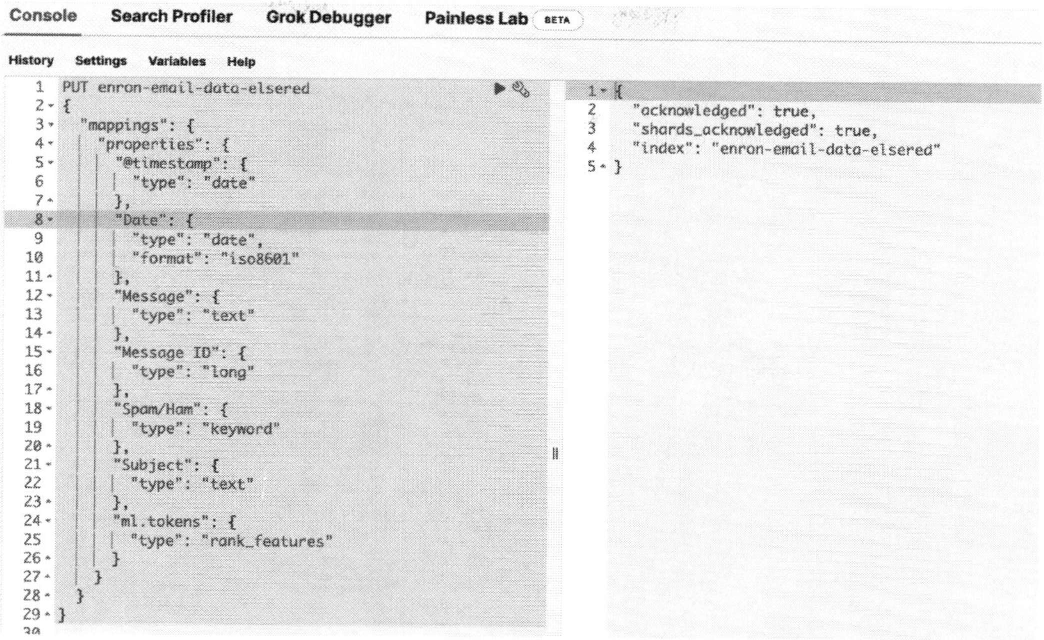

Figure 8.9: New mapping with the rank features field

Now that our destination is ready, we need to build the ingestion pipeline, which will take our initial index data and index it into our new index.

Ingestion pipeline

The ingestion pipeline in this case is fairly simple; it involves taking the right source field and using the right inference from the ELSER model to expand the text and build our token sparse vector. This vector will be saved into the ml.tokens field.

(You can read more about the Ingest Pipeline API here: https://www.elastic.co/guide/en/elasticsearch/reference/current/inference-processor.html.)

To do so, we are going to run the following API, still in **Kibana | Dev Tools**:

```
≡  D  Dev Tools  Console

Console    Search Profiler    Grok Debugger    Painless Lab  BETA

History   Settings   Variables   Help

 32                                                            1 ⌄ {
 33                                                            2    "acknowledged": true
 34   PUT _ingest/pipeline/elser-enron-pipeline    ▶ ✑        3 ⌃ }
 35 ⌄ {
 36 ⌄   "processors": [
 37 ⌄     {
 38 ⌄       "inference": {
 39           "model_id": ".elser_model_1",
 40           "target_field": "ml",
 41 ⌄         "field_map": {
 42             "Message": "text_field"
 43 ⌄         },
 44 ⌄         "inference_config": {
 45 ⌄           "text_expansion": {
 46               "results_field": "tokens"
 47 ⌄           }
 48 ⌄         }
 49 ⌄       }
 50 ⌄     }
 51 ⌄   ]
 52 ⌄ }
 53
```

Figure 8.10: New mapping with the rank features field

The `ingest` processor has two parts:

- `field_map`, which maps the source text field called `Message` in our source index to the `text_field` object expected by the model.

- The `inference` configuration, which leverages the inference ELSER is applying to the data, building the collection of tokens stored in the `ml.tokens` field. These tokens will be used based on the search made by the user later. They are used as a semantic space to compare what the search contains.

We are now ready to reindex the data.

Reindexing the data

We have created our ingestion process, which plays the role of a data mapper between our raw text and what the ELSER model requires to expand the text. We are using a multiple-step approach here, where you first brought the Enron dataset in via the data visualizer and created a pipeline, and are now about to reindex this data into an ELSER-formatted index. You might or might not need to go through this process, depending on whether your data exists in Elasticsearch (in which case, you would use this approach). Otherwise, you can send the data directly to this new index. With that being said, let's take a look at the reindexing process, which does not differ from classic reindexing. It uses our source index and our destination index and leverages the newly created ingest pipeline. Still in **Kibana | Dev Tools**, run the following command to start reindexing the data by batches of 50 documents:

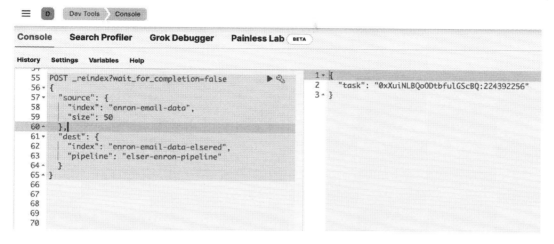

Figure 8.11: Reindexing the Enron data in the ELSER index

You can check the status of the reindexing process via the following call using the task identifier returned by the preceding API call:

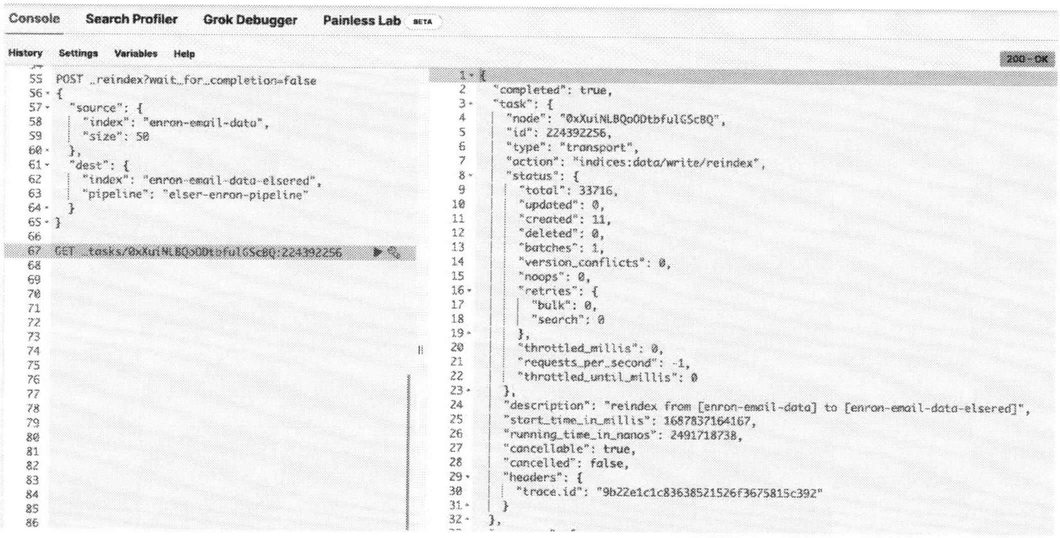

Figure 8.12: Reindexing task status

The preceding API response shows the `completed` field with the `true` value, which means that the reindexing process is done; we should be able to see documents in our newly fed index:

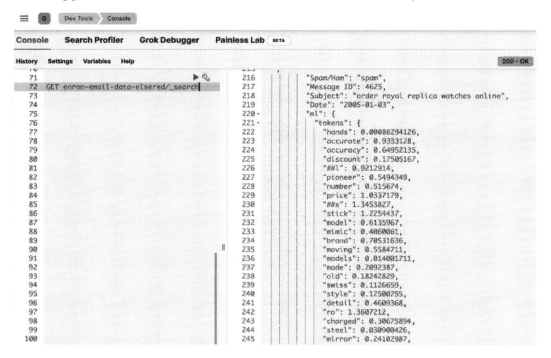

Figure 8.13: Text expansion and created tokens

You can see the expansion happening and this new `ml.tokens` field containing all the tokens created relative to what this specific spam contains. We are now ready to run a semantic search powered by ELSER.

Semantic search with ELSER

With data being properly expanded, we can now run a semantic search using the new `text_expansion` query. We are going to emulate a case in which an email is received and its content or a chunk of its content is sent to Elastic. In a production environment, in reality, the entire email corpus will not be sent to this detector.

Instead, chunks of text extracted from the email can be streamed to Elasticsearch. Each chunk will get a result from the detector. To go further, the score could be aggregated to build an overall score for the set of text chunks streamed using a script.

This might not be the best approach to analyzing an email and seeing whether or not it's a phishing attack, but it has the advantages of isolating the sentence from the rest of the email context and doing a sort of blind test against a referential. It also has the drawback of dissolving the context at the same time.

Let's run an example to illustrate this process. The following is a query that looks at a specific portion of a sentence to see whether it reveals in our reference dataset that spam has been created with the same intent:

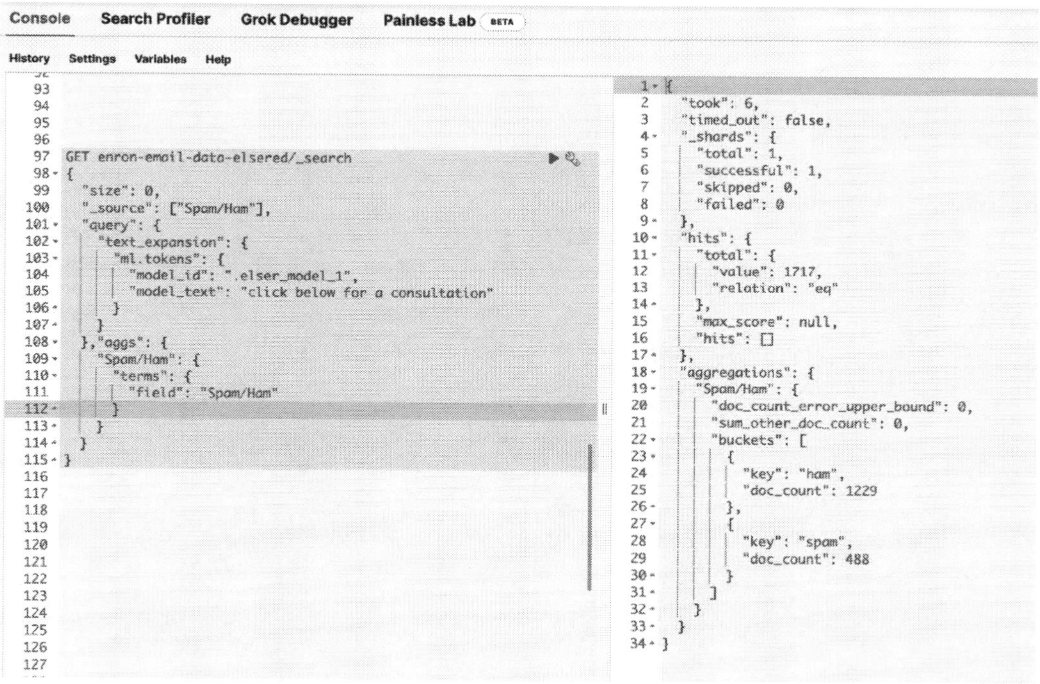

Figure 8.14: Semantic search using the text_expansion query

The semantic search here reveals that out of the 1,677 emails that have been selected in our dataset, 448 were spam, which represents a score of 27% just for this specific portion of text. Now, can we conclude that this is spam? Not at this stage.

So, we really have two options:

- We can run a query with the entire email corpus. The challenge with this method is that it will restrict the numbers of similar emails drastically if it's not standard spam.

- Alternatively, we can run the same query here for a different overlapping portion of text and build up a global score.

Regardless of the method used, remember that you are trying to detect the intent of the email against the text similarity here. Either method will give you a score and it's then up to you to set a threshold for quarantining emails based on the score you are getting. In other words, organizations need to set the threshold that makes sense for them to classify an email as spam.

Limitations of ELSER

While ELSER is a powerful tool for semantic search, it's important to be aware of its current limitations. Understanding these limitations can help users make the most of ELSER's capabilities and plan for potential challenges.

One of the key limitations of ELSER is that it currently only considers the first 512 tokens per field. This equates to approximately the first 300–400 words in each field going through an inference pipeline. It's a bit like reading the first few pages of a book and trying to understand the entire story. While you can get a sense of the book's theme and style, you might miss important details that come later. This means that for longer documents, some content may not be considered in the semantic analysis.

Another limitation is the hardware requirement. ELSER requires at least one ML node with a minimum of 4 GB of memory. This might not be an issue for larger organizations with ample resources, but for smaller organizations or individual users, this requirement could pose a challenge.

Furthermore, ELSER is currently in technical preview, meaning it's still being refined and improved. It's like a new car model that's been released for test drives but hasn't yet been finalized for mass production. This means that some features may change in future versions, and the tool is not yet covered by support **Service Level Agreements (SLAs)** of **generally available (GA)** features such as production-level support. ELSER might be GA by the time this book is published.

Despite these limitations, ELSER represents a significant advancement in the field of semantic search. Elastic is actively working on addressing these limitations and enhancing ELSER's capabilities, with plans to promote this feature to GA in a future release. As with any tool, the key to successful use is understanding its strengths and limitations and adapting your approach accordingly.

Another important limitation to note is that ELSER is currently designed to work with English text. This limitation reflects a broader challenge in the field of natural language processing, where many tools and models are primarily designed for English due to the abundance of available training data in this language. However, this focus on English can limit the applicability of these tools in multilingual or non-English contexts.

Elastic is aware of this limitation and has expressed plans to expand ELSER's capabilities to other languages in future versions. This will make ELSER more versatile and useful in a wider range of contexts.

For now, users working with non-English text will need to consider this limitation and explore other tools or approaches that are designed to handle their specific languages. Despite this current limitation, ELSER's focus on semantic understanding represents a significant step forward in the field of text analysis and search.

Summary

In this chapter, we introduced the opportunity to use a pre-trained model called ELSER, which leverages vectors without users having to manage the vectorization process. It's an out-of-the-box model that generates immediate value from a semantic search perspective. We applied ELSER to the challenge of phishing attacks with the task in mind being to limit the impact of such attacks. You should now be able to build your pipeline to load data in Elasticsearch and start building applications that leverage ELSER, whether in cybersecurity or beyond.

In the next chapter, we are going to go a step further in leveraging vectors by building a retrieval augmented generation application.

Part 4:
Innovative Integrations
and Future Directions

The final part of this book looks toward the horizon, exploring innovative integrations and emerging trends in vector search with Elastic. It covers groundbreaking applications such as retrieval augmented generation and the integration of Elastic with AI platforms. These chapters are a window into the future, showcasing the expansive potential and evolving nature of vector search technology.

This part has the following chapters:

- *Chapter 9, Retrieval Augmented Generation with Elastic*
- *Chapter 10, Building an Elastic Plugin for ChatGPT*

9

Retrieval Augmented Generation with Elastic

In this chapter, we will continue on our journey through the world of Elasticsearch and take a deep dive into one of the most advanced and exciting features that Elastic has to offer: **retrieval augmented generation** (**RAG**) search experiences. If you followed along with our previous chapters, you'll be familiar with the **Elastic Learned Sparse EncodeR** (**ELSER**) pre-trained model and the concept of a vector search, which offers you the luxury of semantic understanding in search results. You also learned about the power of **reciprocal rank fusion** (**RRF**) in combining the strengths of lexical and vector searches.

In this chapter, we will take it up a notch by integrating these concepts into a comprehensive pipeline, culminating in the expansion of a **large language model** (**LLM**) with RAG. The goal here is to combine the strengths of lexical, vector, and contextual search to offer the most relevant search results, enhancing the user experience.

We will go over the following topics:

- The fundamental concepts that constitute a RAG

- How to augment ELSER with RRF to combine it with BM25

- Expanding our LLM knowledge with RAG

- Exploring a real-world case study – CookBot, our culinary chatbot assistant

By the end of this chapter, you will be geared up to build a RAG application based on Elasticsearch.

Preparing for RAG-enhanced search with ELSER and RRF

In our continued discussion on semantic search and its various facets, we now turn our attention to the integration of RAG-enhanced search with ELSER and RRF.

Before we dive into the details of the integration of RAG, ELSER, and RRF, it's essential to appreciate the journey and evolution of search methodologies that brought us here.

The journey started with lexical search. This simple yet powerful methodology, which involves matching exact terms, was vastly adopted and capable of delivering reliable results. It laid the foundation for what was to come.

The next leap forward came with the introduction of vector search, adding a new dimension to our understanding of search queries. This technique enabled systems to comprehend the "meaning" or semantic content behind queries, far beyond the capabilities of a basic lexical search.

Elastic RRF further boosted the relevancy of results. This technique cleverly blended the strengths of both lexical and vector search, bringing together the best of both worlds and further refining the quality of search output.

Finally, the most recent and exciting development has been the integration of LLMs into this framework. Grounded with the output from RRF, these models implemented RAG. This ingenious technique leverages the context awareness of LLMs, allowing them to generate precise, relevant content based on the search results.

Figure 9.1 summarizes the aforementioned information:

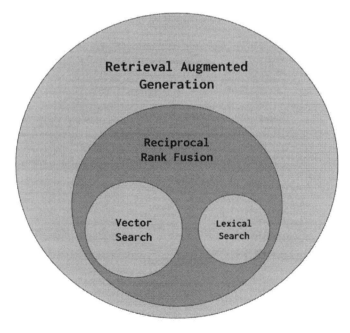

Figure 9.1: The RAG journey

Each step in this journey represents a significant evolution in search technologies. This progressive enhancement has continually improved Elastic's ability to deliver increasingly intelligent, user-centric search experiences.

Now, with this understanding of the evolutionary context, let's delve into the specifics of how RAG, ELSER, and RRF can work together to further advance our search capabilities.

Semantic search with ELSER

As we previously discussed, semantic search has transformed the way we understand and respond to user queries. ELSER is a valuable tool in this sphere, offering a unique way to represent and understand the content and context of user queries in a more in-depth manner.

We previously looked at how ELSER can onboard large content into a high-dimensional token space, creating a semantic map of sorts, to yield more contextually accurate results. However, how does ELSER come into play when we bring in elements such as RAG and RRF? Let's find out.

A recap of essential considerations for RAG

To successfully implement RAG in any search system, there are three key components we must consider: the document store, the retriever, and the generator. These elements interact to form the backbone of an effective RAG-enhanced search system.

Document store

Elasticsearch serves as the document store in our search system, providing the platform where all searchable data resides. This data must be both comprehensive and diverse to accommodate the broad spectrum of information that it may receive from queries. Elasticsearch is known for its ability to handle diverse data types swiftly and efficiently, making it an ideal choice for this role.

Elasticsearch doesn't only act as a passive repository but also plays an active role in delivering a successful search experience. With its powerful full-text search capabilities, efficient indexing, and scalability to handle large volumes of data, Elasticsearch forms a robust foundation to deploy a successful RAG-enhanced search system.

Retriever

The retriever, in this context, operates between the user's query and Elasticsearch, our document store. Here, ELSER, a pre-trained model, plays a pivotal role.

ELSER functions by expanding tokens from the document corpus indexed in Elasticsearch, enhancing its ability to understand and locate semantically relevant information based on user queries. It works hand-in-hand with RRF, a technique that blends lexical search and ELSER-based search.

RRF achieves this by creating sub-queries that assist in combining the precision of lexical search's exact term matching with the enriched semantic understanding offered by ELSER. The integration of these two techniques allows for a more comprehensive and effective retrieval process, significantly boosting the relevance and precision of the search results in our RAG system.

Generator

After the retriever, powered by ELSER and RRF, has identified the most pertinent documents in Elasticsearch, it's the generator's turn to shine. In our setup, the generator is powered by OpenAI's GPT-4, one of the most advanced language models at the time of writing.

GPT-4 uses the output from the retriever to generate detailed, coherent, and contextually relevant text snippets. Harnessing the capabilities of these advanced LLMs, the generator can produce text that directly answers a user's query or provides valuable information related to it.

With the introduction of GPT-4, the text generation process becomes more dynamic and accurate, elevating the semantic search experience to a whole new level. By incorporating GPT-4 into our RAG system, we ensure that the generated responses are not only contextually aligned with the user's query but also maintain a high standard of coherence and relevance.

Remember that while the retriever identifies the relevant "information nuggets" with Elasticsearch, the generator, backed by GPT-4, synthesizes these nuggets into comprehensive and user-friendly responses. Together, these components constitute a robust, intelligent, and effective RAG-enhanced search system, as summarized in the following diagram:

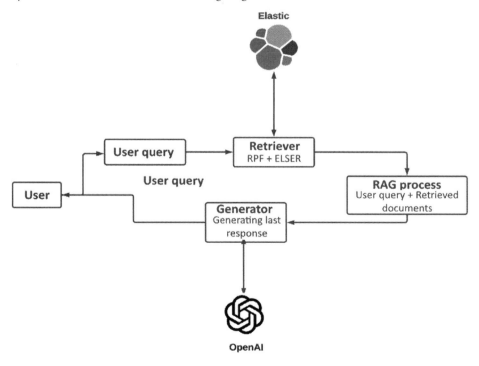

Figure 9.2: RAG search system

It's the interactions and harmony between these components that result in a search experience that is both relevant and contextually rich.

Now that we've reiterated the essential considerations for RAG, we can move on to explore how ELSER plays a significant role in this framework.

Integrating ELSER with RRF

In the *Elastic 8.9* update, the sub-searches feature, which opened new possibilities for search operations, was introduced. This feature is instrumental in integrating ELSER with RRF.

Sub-searches enable multiple distinct search queries to be executed within a single search request. This feature significantly improves the capability to combine different search methodologies.

When integrating ELSER with RRF, the process involves two sub-searches and a fusion step.

BM25 sub-search

Initially, a BM25 sub-search is performed. This sub-query is focused on searching exact or closely related terms from a user's query.

ELSER sub-search

Simultaneously, an ELSER sub-search is carried out. This sub-search captures the contextual subtleties that might be missed in a lexical search.

RRF fusion

Subsequently, the results of the BM25 and ELSER sub-searches are fused using RRF. This method creates a unified list that prioritizes documents identified as relevant by both sub-searches.

This integrative approach allows Elastic to provide a more advanced search experience, not only identifying documents that match search terms but also understanding the underlying user intent and query context.

With the integration of ELSER into RRF via sub-searches, Elastic's search capabilities are set for the next advancement: RAG-enhanced search. In this scenario, the ranked document list produced by the joint efforts of ELSER and RRF is used as a foundational context for a sophisticated language model such as GPT-4, offering even more accurate and intuitive search results.

You can also find much more information about actual relevancy performances in this blog post:

```
https://www.elastic.co/blog/improving-information-retrieval-elastic-
stack-hybrid
```

Language models and RAG

At the time of writing, there are already multiple LLM options available, whether it's paid software, such as OpenAI, or open source ones with free and paid options, such as Meta's newly released Llama 2 (`https://ai.meta.com/llama/`) and Amazon Bedrock (`https://aws.amazon.com/bedrock/`). For the purpose of this chapter, we will use OpenAI's GPT-4.

Pre-trained LLMs

Pre-trained LLMs, such as OpenAI's GPT-4, have been transformative in the field of natural language processing. These models are trained on a vast corpus of text, and through this process, they learn intricate patterns of language, from basic syntax to complex semantic relationships. As a result, they're equipped to generate high-quality, contextually relevant text in response to a given prompt, making them an excellent tool to improve search results.

How RAG expands LLMs

The power of LLMs is harnessed within the RAG framework by employing them in the generation phase. Once the retriever (in our case, a combination of ELSER and RRF) has selected the relevant documents, these documents are used as context by the LLM. The LLM is then prompted with a user's query, generating a response that is not only relevant to the query but also based on the information present in the retrieved documents.

Feeding semantically indexed data to LLMs

To maximize the effectiveness of an LLM in the RAG context, it's crucial to feed it with semantically indexed data. This involves using ELSER to enrich the indexed documents and adding semantic tokens that enhance the document's contextual understanding.

With the incorporation of RRF and ELSER, Elasticsearch can retrieve the most relevant documents based on both lexical search and semantic search. When these documents are provided to the LLM, it takes into account both the user query and the retrieved documents, generating a response that aligns accurately with the search intent. This interaction between RRF, ELSER, and the LLM results in a comprehensive, context-aware, and more precise search experience, which is at the core of RAG-enhanced search.

In-depth case study—implementing a RAG-enhanced CookBot

Everyone knows the age-old culinary dilemma, "*What can I cook with the ingredients I have?*" Many people need help when faced with an array of ingredients but a lack of inspiration or knowledge to whip up a dish. This everyday issue was the spark for our idea—CookBot.

CookBot is not just any AI. It's conceived as an advanced culinary assistant that not only suggests recipes based on the available ingredients but also understands the nuances of user queries, adapts to individual dietary preferences and restrictions, and generates insightful culinary recommendations.

Our objective was to infuse CookBot with RAG, ELSER, and RRF technologies. These technologies are designed to enhance the semantic understanding of queries, optimize information retrieval, and generate relevant, personalized responses. By harnessing the capabilities of these advanced tools, we aimed for CookBot to be able to provide seamless, context-aware culinary assistance tailored to each user's unique needs.

Figure 9.3: CookBot powered by Elastic

Dataset overview – an introduction to the Allrecipes.com dataset

The Allrecipes.com dataset, in its raw CSV format, is a treasure trove of diverse and detailed culinary information. Thus, it is the perfect foundation to train our CookBot. It houses an extensive range of recipes, each encapsulated in a unique entry brimming with an array of information.

You can find and download the dataset here, as it will be used later in the chapter:

https://www.kaggle.com/datasets/nguyentuongquang/all-recipes

To illustrate the richness of this dataset, let's consider a single entry:

```
"group","name","rating","n_rater","n_
reviewer","summary","process","ingredient"
"breakfast-and-brunch.eggs.breakfast-burritos","Ham and Cheese
Breakfast Tortillas",0,0,44,"This is great for a special brunch or
even a quick and easy dinner. Other breakfast meats can be used, but
the deli ham is the easiest since it is already fully cooked.","prep:
30 mins,total: 30 mins,Servings: 4,Yield: 4 servings","12 eggs +
<U+2153> cup milk + 3 slices cooked ham, diced + 2 green onions,
minced + salt and pepper to taste + 4 ounces Cheddar cheese, shredded
+ 4 (10 inch) flour tortillas +  cup salsa"
```

Each entry in the dataset represents a unique recipe and encompasses various fields:

- group: This is the categorization of the recipe. It provides a general idea about the type and nature of the dish.

- name: This is the title or name of the recipe. This field straightforwardly tells us what the dish is.

- rating and n_rater: These fields indicate the popularity and approval of the dish among users.

- n_reviewer: This is the number of users who have reviewed the recipe.

- summary: This is a brief overview or description of the dish, often providing valuable context about its taste, usage, or preparation.

- process: This field outlines crucial details such as preparation time, total cooking time, servings, and yield.

- ingredient: This is a comprehensive list of all the ingredients required for the recipe, along with their quantities.

The detailed information offered by each field gives us a broad and varied information space, aiding the retriever in navigating the data and ensuring the generator can accurately respond to a diverse range of culinary queries. As we move forward, we will discuss how we indexed this dataset using Elasticsearch, the role of ELSER and RRF in effectively retrieving data, and how the GPT-4 model generates relevant, personalized responses based on the retrieved data.

Preparing data for RAG-enhanced search

To transform the Allrecipes.com data into a searchable database, we first need to parse the CSV file and subsequently create an Elasticsearch index where data will be stored and queried. Let's walk through this process implemented as part of the Python code.

Connecting to Elasticsearch

First, we need to establish a connection with our Elasticsearch instance. This connection is handled by the Elasticsearch object from the Elasticsearch Python module:

```
from elasticsearch import Elasticsearch
es = Elasticsearch()
```

In this case, we assume that our Elasticsearch instance runs locally with default settings. If it doesn't, we will need to provide the appropriate host and port information to the Elasticsearch class.

Defining the index

The next step is to define an index where our recipes will be stored. An index in Elasticsearch is like a database in traditional database systems. In this case, we'll call our index `recipes`:

```
index_name = 'recipes'
```

Creating the mapping

Now, we need to create a mapping for our index. A mapping is like a schema in a SQL database and defines the types of each field in the documents that will be stored in the index. We will define a mapping as a Python dictionary:

```
mapping = {
    "mappings": {
        "properties": {
            "group": { "type": "text" },
            "name": { "type": "text" },
            "rating": { "type": "text" },
            "n_rater": { "type": "text" },
            "n_reviewer": { "type": "text" },
            "summary": {
                "type": "text",
                "analyzer": "english"
            },
            "process": { "type": "text" },
            "ingredient": {
                "type": "text",
            },
            "ml.tokens": {
                "type": "rank_features"
            }
        }
    }
}
```

Here, all fields are defined as text, which means they are full-text searchable. We also specify that the `summary` field should be analyzed using the English analyzer, which will help to optimize searches in English text by taking into account things such as stemming and stop words. Finally, we create the field that ELSER will use to create the token set, which is the result of the expansion happening based on the terms passed to ELSER.

Creating the index

Once we've defined our mapping, we can create the index in Elasticsearch with the following:

```
es.indices.create(index=index_name, body=mapping)
```

This sends a request to Elasticsearch to create an index with the specified name and mapping.

Reading the CSV file

With our index ready, we can now read our dataset from the CSV file. We'll use `pandas`, a powerful data manipulation library in Python, to do this:

```
import pandas as pd
with open('recipe_dataset.csv', 'r', encoding='utf-8',
errors='ignore') as file:
    df = pd.read_csv(file)
```

This code opens the CSV file and reads it into a `pandas` dataframe, a two-dimensional tabular data structure that's perfect for manipulating structured data.

Converting to dictionaries

To index the data into Elasticsearch, we need to convert our dataframe into a list of dictionaries, where each dictionary corresponds to a row (i.e., a document or recipe) in the dataframe:

```
recipes = df.to_dict('records')
print(f"Number of documents: {len(recipes)}")
```

At this point, we have our dataset ready to index in Elasticsearch. However, considering the size of the dataset, it is advisable to use the bulk indexing feature for efficient data ingestion. This will be covered in the next section.

Bulk indexing the data

Let's look into the step-by-step process of bulk indexing your dataset in Elasticsearch.

Defining the preprocessing pipeline

Before we proceed to bulk indexing, we need to set up a pipeline to preprocess the documents. Here, we will use the `elser-v1-recipes` pipeline, which utilizes the ELSER model for semantic indexing. The pipeline is defined as follows:

```
[
  {
    "inference": {
      "model_id": ".elser_model_1",
```

```
      "target_field": "ml",
      "field_map": {
        "ingredient": "text_field"
      },
      "inference_config": {
        "text_expansion": {
          "results_field": "tokens"
        }
      }
    }
  }
]
```

The pipeline includes an `inference` processor that uses the ELSER pre-trained model to perform semantic indexing. It maps the `ingredient` field from the recipe data to the `text_field` object of the ELSER model. The output (the expanded tokens from the ELSER model) is stored in the `tokens` field under the `ml` field in the document.

Creating a bulk indexing sequence

Given the size of the `Allrecipes.com` dataset, it's impractical to index each document individually. Instead, we can utilize Elasticsearch's bulk API, which allows us to index multiple documents in a single request. First, we need to generate a list of dictionaries, where each dictionary corresponds to a bulk index operation:

```
bulk_index_body = []
for index, recipe in enumerate(recipes):
    document = {
        "_index": "recipes",
        "pipeline": "elser-v1-recipes",
        "_source": recipe
    }
    bulk_index_body.append(document)
```

In this loop, we iterate over each recipe (a dictionary) in our `recipes` list and then construct a new dictionary with the necessary information for the bulk index operation. This dictionary specifies the name of the index where the document will be stored (`recipes`), the ingest pipeline to be used to process the document (`elser-v1-recipes`), and the document source itself (`recipe`).

Performing the bulk index operation

With our `bulk_index_body` array ready, we can now perform the bulk index operation:

```
try:
    response = helpers.bulk(es, bulk_index_body, chunk_size=500,
request_timeout=60*3)
    print ("\nRESPONSE:", response)
except BulkIndexError as e:
    for error in e.errors:
        print(f"Document ID: {error['index']['_id']}")
        print(f"Error Type: {error['index']['error']['type']}")
        print(f"Error Reason: {error['index']['error']['reason']}")
```

We use the `helpers.bulk()` function from the Elasticsearch library to provide our Elasticsearch connection (`es`)—the `bulk_index_body` array we just created—with a `chunk_size` value of `500` (which specifies that we want to send 500 documents per request) and a `request_timeout` value of `180` seconds, which specifies that we want to allow each request to take up to 3 minutes before timing out because the indexing could take a long time with ELSER.

The `helpers.bulk()` function will return a response indicating the number of operations attempted and the number of errors, if any.

If any errors occur during the bulk index operation, these will be raised as `BulkIndexError`. We can catch this exception and iterate over its `errors` attribute to get information about each individual error, including the ID of the document that caused the error, the type of error, and the reason for it.

At the end of this process, you will have successfully indexed your entire `Allrecipes.com` dataset in Elasticsearch, ready for it to be retrieved and processed by your RAG-enhanced CookBot.

Building the retriever—RRF with ELSER

In the context of our recipe retrieval task, our goal is to maximize the relevance of the returned recipes based on a user's query. We will utilize a combination of classic full-text search (via BM25), semantic search (with ELSER), and a robust rank fusion method (RRF). This combination allows us to handle more complex queries and return results that align closely with the user's intent.

Let's consider the following query:

```
GET recipes/_search
{
  "_source": { "includes": [ "name", "ingredient" ] },
  "sub_searches": [
    {
      "query": {
        "bool": {
```

```
                "must": { "match": {
"ingredient": "carrot beef" } },
            "must_not": { "match": { "ingredient": "onion" }
            }
          }
        }
      },
      {
        "query": {
          "text_expansion": { "ml.tokens": {
              "model_id": ".elser_model_1",
              "model_text": "I want a recipe from the US west coast with
beef"
            }
          }
        }
      }
    ],
    "rank": {
      "rrf": { "window_size": 50, "rank_constant": 20 }
    }
}
```

This query includes two types of search. The first uses a classic Elasticsearch Boolean search to find recipes that contain both carrot and beef as ingredients, excluding those with onion. This traditional approach ensures that the most basic constraints of the user are met.

The second sub_search employs ELSER to semantically expand the query I want a recipe from the US west coast with beef. ELSER interprets this request based on its understanding of language, enabling the system to match documents that may not contain the exact phrase but are contextually related. This allows the system to factor in the more nuanced preferences of the user.

The query then employs RRF to combine the results of the two sub_searches. The window_size parameter is set to 50, meaning the top 50 results from each sub-search are considered. The rank_constant parameter, set to 20, guides the RRF algorithm to fuse the scores from the two sub_searches.

Thus, this query exemplifies the effective combination of BM25, ELSER, and RRF. Exploiting the strengths of each allows CookBot to move beyond simple keyword matches and provide more contextually relevant recipes, improving the user experience and increasing the system's overall utility.

Leveraging the retriever and implementing the generator

Now that we have our Elasticsearch retriever set up and ready to go, let's proceed with the final part of our RAG system: the generator. In the context of our application, we'll use the GPT-4 model as the generator. We'll implement the generator in our `recipe_generator.py` module and then integrate it into our Streamlit application.

Building the generator

We will start by creating a `RecipeGenerator` class. This class is initialized with an OpenAI API key (find out how to get an OpenAI key at https://help.openai.com/en/articles/4936850-where-do-i-find-my-secret-api-key), which is used to authenticate our requests with the GPT-4 model:

```python
import openai
import json
from config import OPENAI_API_KEY

class RecipeGenerator:
    def __init__(self, api_key):
        self.api_key = api_key
        openai.api_key = self.api_key


Next, we define the generate function in the RecipeGenerator class.
This function takes in a recipe as input, and sends it as a prompt to
the GPT-4 model, asking it to generate a detailed, step-by-step guide.

def generate(self, recipe):
    prompts = [{"role": "user", "content": json.dumps(recipe)}]
    instruction = {
        "role": "system",
        "content": "Take the recipes information and generate a recipe
with a mouthwatering intro and a step by step guide."
    }
    prompts.append(instruction)

    generated_content = openai.ChatCompletion.create(
        model="gpt-4",
        messages=prompts,
        max_tokens=1000
    )
    return generated_content.choices[0].message.content
```

The prompts are formatted as required by the OpenAI API, and the `max_tokens` parameter is set to `1000` to limit the length of the generated text. The generated recipe is then returned by the function.

Integrating the generator into the Streamlit application

With our `RecipeGenerator` class ready, we can now integrate it into our Streamlit application in `main.py`. After importing the necessary modules and initializing the `RecipeGenerator` class, we will set up the user interface with a text input field:

```python
from recipe_generator import RecipeGenerator
from config import OPENAI_API_KEY
generator = RecipeGenerator(OPENAI_API_KEY)
input_text = st.text_input(" ", placeholder="Ask me anything about cooking")
```

When the user enters a query, we will use the Elasticsearch retriever to get a relevant recipe. We then pass this recipe to the `generate` function of `RecipeGenerator`, and the resulting text is displayed in the Streamlit application (see a video example at `https://www.linkedin.com/posts/bahaaldine_genai-gpt4-elasticsearch-activity-7091802199315394560-TkPY`):

```python
if input_text:
    query = {
        "sub_searches": [
            {
                "query": {
                    "bool": {
                        "must_not": [
                            {
                                "match": {
                                    "ingredient": "onion"
                                }
                            }
                        ]
                    }
                }
            },
            {
                "query": {
                    "text_expansion": {
                        "ml.tokens": {
                            "model_id": ".elser_model_1",
                            "model_text": input_text
                        }
                    }
                }
            }
        ],
        "rank": {
            "rrf": {
```

```
                        "window_size": 50,
                        "rank_constant": 20
                }
        }
    }
recipe = elasticsearch_query(query)
st.write(recipe)
st.write(generator.generate(recipe))
```

The generator thus works in tandem with the retriever to provide a detailed, step-by-step recipe based on the user's query. This completes our implementation of the RAG system in a Streamlit application, bridging the gap between retrieving relevant information and generating coherent, meaningful responses.

Summary

After a deep exploration of the numerous technicalities and advanced methods involved in building CookBot, we can conclude that the application of RAG, ELSER, BM25, and RRF has significantly contributed to CookBot's unique ability to answer culinary queries with enhanced precision and depth.

Throughout the course of this chapter, we've uncovered the potential of RAG as a retriever for finding relevant documents and as a generator for crafting detailed responses. By incorporating ELSER and BM25, the retrieval component gains the advantage of both semantic context and keyword efficiency. The fusion of these retrieval methods with RRF leads to the curation of a highly relevant set of recipes, even when faced with complex or vague queries.

The integration of RAG into CookBot's architecture has further amplified its capabilities, demonstrating the value of an iterative approach where knowledge is refined over multiple steps. By employing GPT-4 as the generator in the RAG setup, CookBot is capable of producing diverse, rich, and contextually accurate responses.

With the utilization of the `Allrecipes.com` dataset as the base and the well-coordinated use of RAG, ELSER, BM25, and RRF, we have managed to create CookBot, a bot that can expertly navigate the culinary space and provide personalized assistance. This model serves as an illustration of how combining state-of-the-art retrieval methods with powerful language models can yield practical and efficient solutions for diverse domains.

As we move forward, we can anticipate further enhancements and refinements to CookBot, demonstrating the endless possibilities in the realm of AI-driven culinary assistance. This exploration has served as a primer for us to dive into more advanced techniques and strategies that can be employed to create powerful conversational AI systems.

We hope you have gained a comprehensive understanding of these key concepts and their applications to gain a deeper appreciation for the fascinating field of AI. In the next chapter, we will tackle the ChatGPT plugin framework and extend our acquired knowledge about RAG to integrate directly into the ChatGPT experience.

10

Building an Elastic Plugin for ChatGPT

Context is the backbone of understanding. It's paramount that conversational AI systems such as ChatGPT are updated with the most recent information to stay relevant in the rapidly changing technological landscape. While a static knowledge base can address a broad array of questions, the precision and relevance of answers can be significantly enhanced when the system understands the present context.

The **Dynamic Context Layer (DCL)** offers a solution. By continuously updating the model's knowledge with the latest data, the DCL ensures that the AI's responses are not just accurate but also timely and context-aware. This chapter focuses on creating such a layer for ChatGPT using Elasticsearch's vector capabilities combined with Embedchain, a framework designed to effortlessly craft LLM-powered bots over any dataset. Our primary objective is to enable ChatGPT to pull and comprehend the latest domain-specific information, ensuring it delivers the most current answers to user queries.

In this chapter, we will cover the following topics:

- Importance of context in large language models

- The concept of Significance of Context

- Embedchain as a framework for creating LLM-powered bots over different datasets

- How to build a ChatGPT plugin for Elasticsearch

As we progress, we'll evaluate our system. How does ChatGPT, now armed with the most recent Elastic context, respond to user queries? What difference does a dynamic, up-to-date dataset make?

By the end of this chapter, you will not only understand the mechanics behind building a DCL, but you'll also gain an appreciation for the value of providing your conversational AI with a live, ever-updating data source.

Contextual foundations

The contextual foundations set the stage for our journey as we revisit the importance of **context** in the realm of **large language models** (**LLMs**). In this brief section, we'll understand why maintaining a relevant and dynamic context is paramount for meaningful interactions, especially in applications where the content is ever-evolving. This foundational knowledge will provide the basis for the innovations we'll explore in the subsequent sections.

The paradigm of dynamic context

In any conversation, the richness and relevance of a response often hinges on the context in which it's given. As we've journeyed through this book, we've come to appreciate the vast knowledge repositories that LLMs such as GPT draw from. But what happens when we want our model to grasp the nuances of fresh data? This section introduces the concept of dynamic context—its significance, its challenges, and the potential it brings to modern chatbots. We will delve into the rationale behind dynamically augmenting ChatGPT's responses using up-to-date data, setting the stage for the more technical explorations that follow.

The evolution of Significance of Context in large language models

When we discuss context in relation to large language models such as ChatGPT, we aren't solely referring to the user's immediate input. Context is a combination of implicit and explicit signals that shape a model's output, ensuring its responses align with the overarching dialogue's theme and specific nuances.

LLMs such as GPT-4, through extensive training on a wide range of datasets, have developed an innate understanding of context. These vast training sessions have equipped them with the ability to generate human-like text informed by patterns discerned during their training. Simply put, they've learned to mimic how humans converse by studying countless conversations.

A defining trait of ChatGPT is its operation on a rolling window of context. By prioritizing recent interactions to inform their next responses, they ensure that the flow of a conversation is maintained. If a user suddenly shifts topics or circles back to a previous point, the LLM responds appropriately due to this contextual window. It's what makes a conversation with ChatGPT, or similar models, feel continuous rather than disjointed.

Why static knowledge isn't enough—the advantages of a dynamic context

When we converse with humans, we rely heavily on the most recent and relevant information available to us. Our decisions, insights, and discussions aren't solely based on memories from years ago; they incorporate the latest news, recent experiences, and updated knowledge. LLMs, in their essence, should strive to mimic this aspect of human conversation. Yet, when restricted to static knowledge, their potential is stifled.

Let's see why:

- **Outdated information**: Static knowledge represents a snapshot in time. No matter how vast or detailed this snapshot might be, it will inevitably become outdated. For example, a static model might be well-versed in the features of a software application as of its last update. But what about the new features or modifications added after? Users seeking the latest information would find the static knowledge to be incomplete or, worse, misleading.

- **Loss of relevance**: The information that was deemed relevant or essential a few years, months, or even weeks ago might not hold the same significance today. Trends evolve, global situations change, and user interests shift. A dynamic context ensures that the data being accessed aligns with the current situation, maintaining its relevance to the user.

- **Inability to address recent developments**: From technological advancements to global events, the world is in a state of constant flux. Without the ability to tap into a dynamic context, LLMs are left in the dark about these developments, rendering them incapable of addressing questions or topics that pertain to recent events.

- **The depth of static databases**: While static databases can be vast, they don't grow or evolve in real time. They might have deep knowledge of specific subjects but lack the breadth needed to address newer, interdisciplinary topics.

The power of dynamic context

Contrary to the limitations of static knowledge, dynamic context offers an ever-evolving knowledge base. Let's now see the advantages of dynamic context:

- **Real-time updates**: With a connection to live data sources or current databases, the information provided is always updated. Users get answers that reflect the most recent state of knowledge on a given topic.

- **Increased relevance**: Dynamic context allows LLMs to tap into current trends, discussions, and global happenings. This ensures that the answers provided align closely with what's relevant in the present moment.

- **Scalability**: As the world grows and evolves, so does the dynamic context. It scales with the influx of new data, ensuring a continuously expanding knowledge base.

- **Interactivity**: By being in sync with the current context, LLMs can offer more interactive and engaging conversations. They can respond to real-time events, provide updates on ongoing situations, or even react to new trends, much like a well-informed human can.

In essence, while static knowledge provides a solid foundation, it's the dynamic context that breathes life into LLMs, transforming them from mere repositories of information to entities capable of meaningful, current, and interactive dialogues.

Significance of Context

To introduce the concept of the **Significance of Context** (**SoC**), consider the following analogy that leverages the example we built in *Chapter 9, Retrieval Augmented Generation with Elastic*.

Imagine using a recipe app to prepare dinner. Initially, you only have access to recipes from a single, dated cookbook. While the recipes provide a basic foundation, they might not cater to today's dietary preferences or use ingredients currently in your pantry.

A week later, the app gets an upgrade. Now, it not only includes recipes from multiple sources but can also adjust them based on user reviews, seasonality of ingredients, and your personal dietary restrictions. Furthermore, each time you use it, the app learns from your choices and starts suggesting recipes that are likely to fit your taste profile.

Let's tie this to the factors of context significance:

- **Relevance** (**R**): The initial broad range of recipes was of general relevance, but after learning your specific preferences, the app's suggestions became highly relevant to your tastes. You receive an enhanced user experience with the help of personalization.

- **Continuity** (**C**): As you continually provide the app with feedback on your dietary preferences, there's consistency in the type of recipes you see, offering a continuous stream of tailored suggestions.

- **Timeliness** (**T**): The app also takes into account the season and the latest cooking trends. By doing so, it ensures that the recipes suggested are timely, making use of seasonal ingredients and aligning with current culinary trends.

- **Accuracy** (**A**): By syncing with verified culinary sources and integrating user reviews, the app ensures that its recipe suggestions are not just popular but also accurate in terms of ingredients, proportions, and cooking methods. The combination of the LLM with a context will help minimize the LLM hallucinations. LLM hallucination is when an LLM presents false, fabricated, or nonsensical information, mostly due to a misunderstanding of information or biased information in the training dataset.

Much like our objective with the DCL for the Elastic documentation in ChatGPT, we aim to ensure that the information provided isn't just accurate but also highly relevant, continuous, and timely for the user's needs.

The SoC, akin to relevancy scoring in search engines, could serve as a quantifiable measure to evaluate the efficiency and accuracy of a language model's context-awareness. In this book, we want to take a stab at creating a mathematical representation of SoC. Given the aforementioned factors, here is a possible representation:

$$SoC = \frac{1}{(1 + e^{-k(w_r \cdot R + w_c \cdot C + w_t \cdot T + w_a \cdot A - threshold_j)})}$$

In the preceding formula, the weights are as follows:

- w_R = weight for relevance
- w_C = weight for continuity
- w_T = weight for timeliness
- w_A = weight for accuracy

threshold in this context would be the adjusted value (typically the sum of the weights) that ensures the mid-point of the sigmoid function aligns with the desired balance point of the parameters. The sigmoid function is utilized to bind the SoC between 0 and 1, ensuring it represents a percentage or a probability-like measure of the context's significance.

For instance, in a real-time news bot, timeliness might have a heavier weight, while for a tech support bot, relevance and accuracy could be more significant.

To make this actionable, each of the scores (*R*, *C*, *T*, and *A*) should ideally be between 0 and 1, with 1 being the best possible score.

Data for these scores could be obtained through user feedback, direct evaluation, or other metrics such as the time taken for follow-up questions (indicating potential confusion or lack of clarity).

Over time, as more data are gathered, the weights can be adjusted to better reflect user needs and preferences.

The role of k in the sigmoid function

k determines the steepness of the sigmoid curve.

Increasing *k* makes the sigmoid function steeper, meaning SoC becomes less sensitive to average performances and more discerning of exceptional ones.

Decreasing *k* softens the curve, allowing even small changes in the input scores to affect the SoC noticeably.

By evaluating the SoC, it's possible to not only assess the performance of the language model but also identify areas for improvement. It also provides an actionable way to enhance the model iteratively. Having explored the significance and necessity of dynamic context, let's delve into how we can implement it. Next, we'll examine the architecture and flow of the DCL plugin, illustrating the bridge between theory and application.

Example

Let's try to see why having a data store—that is, not only a vector database but also a search engine capable of delivering the most relevant search results—is important. The following code shows how to plot the SoC when relevancy is driving it:

```python
# Import necessary libraries
import numpy as np
import matplotlib.pyplot as plt
# Define the SoC function using sigmoid
def soc_function(R, C, T, A, k=1, threshold=2):
return 1 / (1 + np.exp(-k*(R + C + T + A - threshold)))
# Sample R, C, T, A values
R_values = np.linspace(0.8, 1, 50)
C_values = np.linspace(0.8, 1, 50)
T_values = np.linspace(0.8, 1, 50)
A_values = np.linspace(0.8, 1, 50)
# Compute SoC values for the sample R, C, T, A values
soc_values = soc_function(R_values, C_values, T_values, A_values)

# Plotting the function
plt.figure(figsize=(10, 6))
plt.plot(R_values, soc_values, label="SoC values", color='blue')
plt.axhline(y=0.5, color='r', linestyle='--', label="Midpoint")
plt.title("Significance of Context (SoC) vs. R (with C, T, A held
constant)")
plt.xlabel("Relevance (R)")
plt.ylabel("SoC Value")
plt.legend()
plt.grid(True)
plt.show()
```

The preceding code would plot the following:

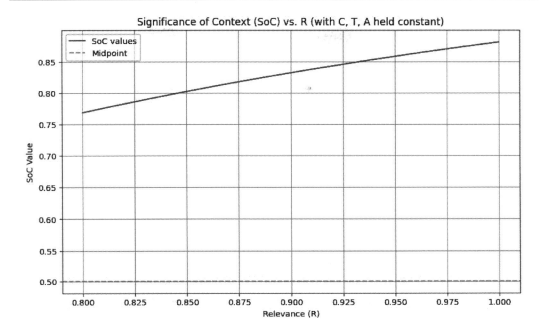

Figure 10.1: Significance of Context measure as a function of relevancy with C, T, and A held constant

Elasticsearch comes with the significant advantage that it enables the users to fine-tune the relevancy. This plot shows that despite there being three factors in addition to relevancy that make up the SoC, the more controls on relevancy the data store gives, the more the significance of the dynamic context will increase.

Dynamic Context Layer plugin vision—architecture and flow

In this section, we get to the heart of our project: the design and flow of the DCL plugin. We'll lay out its structure, explaining how ChatGPT, Embedchain, and Elasticsearch work together. By understanding the underlying architecture and the steps of data flow, you'll see how to integrate real-time data into a chatbot's responses. We'll discuss why certain design choices were made and their impact on the system's functionality.

In any advanced system, clarity of structure and function is crucial. The DCL is no exception. To navigate through the mechanics of how ChatGPT interacts with Elasticsearch via Embedchain, we must first familiarize ourselves with the foundational components enabling this integration. Each component serves a unique purpose, collectively enabling our chatbot to dynamically retrieve, comprehend, and relay current information.

Central to the DCL are three primary components: the **Vector Search Engine** (**VSE**), the **Semantic Embedding Generator** (**SEG**), and the **Conversational Engine** (**CE**). Far from being isolated units, these components are intricately linked, ensuring that our chatbot's insights are not only accurate but also timely and contextually relevant.

As we progress deeper into this chapter, these components will act as our navigational beacons, guiding us through the architecture and flow of the DCL system. Let's embark on this journey by first understanding each of these foundational pillars.

The following diagram is a visual representation of the DCL system, showcasing how each core component interacts to provide a seamless and dynamic conversational experience:

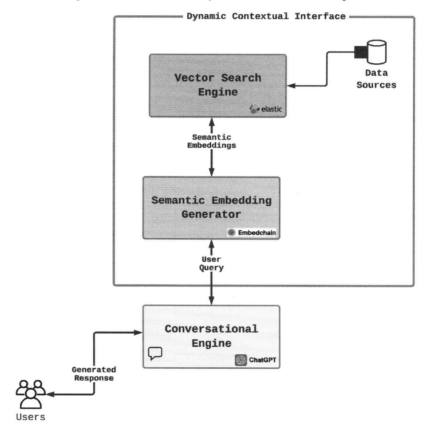

Figure 10.2: The system architecture of the Dynamic Context Layer

The **Dynamic Contextual Interface** (**DCI**) serves as the central hub, orchestrating the flow of information and interactions between the chatbot and the VSE. It's a multifaceted interface designed to understand, interpret, and translate the requests and responses between the Conversational Engine and the underlying data repository. On the other hand, the **Real-Time Contextual Fetcher** (**RCF**) embodies the dynamic aspect of this entire system. As the name suggests, the RCF is responsible for actively retrieving the most recent and relevant information from the VSE. Whether it's pulling the latest documentation updates or extracting vector-embedded insights, the RCF ensures that the data fed to the chatbot is always current, making the conversation as relevant and informed as possible. Together, the DCI and RCF form the active link that binds the static and dynamic worlds of data and conversation.

After establishing a clear understanding of the DCL plugin's architecture, it's time to transition from the blueprint to the construction phase. In the following section, we'll detail the steps and considerations for building the dynamic layer, ensuring our ChatGPT can effectively utilize Elasticsearch and Embedchain for real-time context adaptation.

Building the DCL

In this section, we will embark on the tangible steps of constructing our envisioned tool. We'll dive deep into the technicalities of merging Elasticsearch's capabilities with Embedchain, focusing on the practical aspects of implementing and optimizing this integration with ChatGPT. By the end of this section, you'll have a comprehensive understanding of how to make this DCL operational and how to fine-tune its performance for optimal user experience.

Fetching the latest information from Elastic documentation

Let's now dive into the practical side of our exploration. Here, we'll discuss how to source the most recent documentation from Elastic, a crucial step in ensuring our dynamic context is up to date. This process serves as the initial step in populating our context with relevant and timely data, laying the groundwork for ChatGPT to interact in a context-aware manner.

Data extraction is a foundational step in the creation of our DCL. There are different options to onboard data in Elastic; here we will use the Elastic web crawler. The crawler enables users, with only a URL, to start ingesting data from a website. With the Elastic web crawler, we have a simplified and direct way of acquiring the necessary data. The advantages of the web crawler are as follows:

- **Simple setup**: Instead of constructing elaborate data integration pipelines or dealing with varied content sources, the Elastic web crawler requires only a URL to start its extraction process.

- **Direct integration with Elasticsearch**: After activation, the crawler directly fetches data and feeds it into an Elasticsearch index. This seamless process ensures that the data is readily available for the subsequent stages without delays.

- **Configurability**: The tool is versatile. While the default configuration is sufficient for many scenarios, it's possible to customize the crawl, either by focusing on specific parts of a website or adjusting how often it checks for new content.

For our specific requirement, fetching the Elastic documentation use case from `https://www.elastic.co/guide`, the Elastic web crawler is essential. It methodically scans the guide, ensuring a thorough capture of the most recent documentation. This data, once indexed in Elasticsearch, is primed for semantic embeddings and subsequent interactions with ChatGPT.

With tools such as the Elastic web crawler, we can worry less about how to gather data and focus more on how to effectively utilize this data to enhance our chatbot's performance.

Let's first start by making sure you are running an Enterprise Search node in your Elastic Cloud deployment:

1. Open your deployment and check whether you see a node like that shown in the following screenshot:

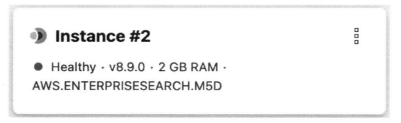

Figure 10.3: Enterprise Search node in the Elastic Cloud console

2. If not, then you need to edit your deployment to add one. Click on the **Edit** button on the left-hand side:

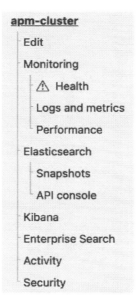

Figure 10.4: Side menu in the Elastic Cloud console

3. Scroll down and add an Enterprise Search instance with the following settings:

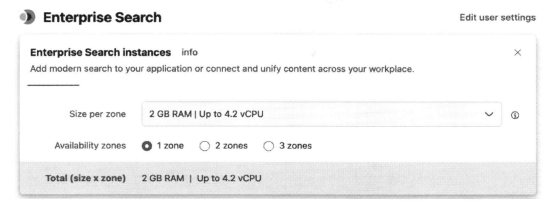

Figure 10.5: Enterprise Search instance configuration

4. Update your deployment. Once finished, navigate to your Kibana instance, then to the **Search** section under **Content/Indices**. From there, you should see a **Create an Index** button, as shown in the following screenshot:

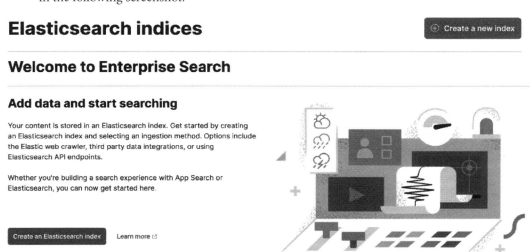

Figure 10.6: Enterprise Search add data assistant

5. Click on this button and choose **Use a web crawler** (link to the known issues: https://www. elastic.co/guide/en/enterprise-search/current/crawler-known-issues.html) from the options that appear:

Select an ingestion method

Create a search optimized Elasticsearch index to store your content. Start by selecting an ingestion method.

View additional integrations

Figure 10.7: Ingestion method selection

6. Name your index—here, I used the name `packt-cdl-source`:

Web crawler search index

Use the web crawler to programmatically discover, extract, and index searchable content from websites and knowledge bases.

Create an Elasticsearch index

This index will hold your data source content, and is optimized with default field mappings for relevant search experiences. Give your index a unique name and optionally set a default language analyzer ⟲ for the index.

Figure 10.8: Web crawler search index creation

7. In the **Domain URL** field, add `https://www.elastic.co`, as this is the one we want to crawl:

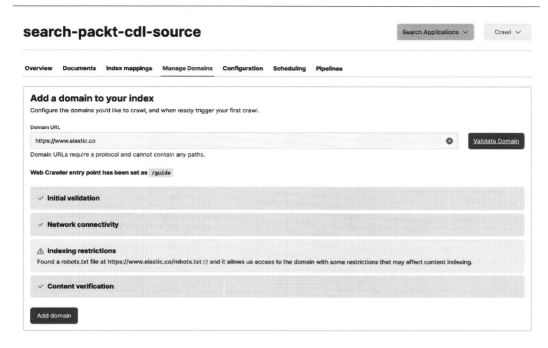

Figure 10.9: Crawler domain validation

8.   Since we only want to crawl the documentation, add the /guide entry point:

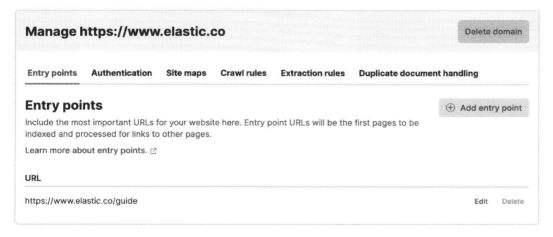

Figure 10.10: Crawler entry points

Then, start crawling all domains by clicking on the **Crawl** button in the top right:

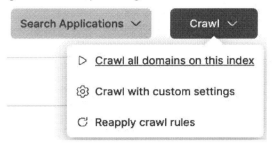

Figure 10.11: Crawler actions

9. You can verify whether the documents are coming in by running the GET search-packt-cdl-source/_search query through Dev Tools.

The good news is that we don't have to do any transformations or data processing to be able to use these documents with Embedchain. Instead, we are going to focus on the URL field of these documents, as this is key to building our pluggable DCL.

Elevating data with Embedchain

In this section, we dive deep into the mechanics of Embedchain (https://github.com/embedchain/embedchain), an open source data platform designed to supercharge datasets with LLM capabilities. We'll explore how it seamlessly integrates with Elasticsearch, enabling ChatGPT to comprehend and respond based on the enhanced semantic context of the dataset. This section provides both the *how* and the *why* behind leveraging Embedchain to bridge the gap between raw data and meaningful interactions.

We like to think of Embedchain as another abstraction layer on top of LangChain, vector databases, and LLMs. It offers a higher level of control and is purpose-built to load context in LLMs from different types of data sources. The closest example I can think of is in the film *The Matrix*, when Trinity asks for a helicopter training program and Tank loads it into her mind. Embedchain pretty much works on the same level of simplicity. Here is an example:

```
elastic_bot.add(" https://jobs.elastic.co/jobs/csm/san-
francisco-ca/customer-architect/5112073?gh_jid=5112073#/")
```

This will load a page containing a job description into an Embedchain application called elastic_bot so that when users submit questions about this role, the elastic_bot application will have the context:

```
elastic_bot.query("Tell me about  the Customer Architect role at
Elastic")
```

This is what the Embedchain bot output looks like for this example:

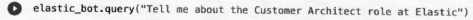

```
elastic_bot.query("Tell me about the Customer Architect role at Elastic")
```

'The Customer Architect role at Elastic is a position within the Customer Success Group. Customer Architects at Elastic are responsible for working with customers to understand their needs and requirements, and then designing and implementing s olutions using Elastic's technology stack. They help customers optimize their use of Elastic's products for search, observability, and security purposes. Customer Architects also provide technical guidance and support to customers throughout th e implementation process.'

Figure 10.12: Embedchain output

It is as simple as that! So, let's put this into the context of our goal. We want the user to interact through ChatGPT with our plugin that, in response to a prompt, will load the correct documentation page via Embedchain. When an Embedchain application adds content, it actually stores it in an underlying vector database. It uses OpenAI's *Ada* embedding model to create the embeddings out of the chunk of data that it scraped. All the chunking and hydration of the data is done by Embedchain.

In this example, we will use Elasticsearch as a vector database. The following code block shows the structure of the document indexed by Embedchain when a link is added:

```
{
        "_index": "embedchain_store_1536",
        "_id":
"635ef64b5a99725d3b2cdf1cca86d5570a70388aa4d8d328cb2a02dd74b232c8",
        "_score": 1,
        "_source": {
            "text": "Aligning with customer business goals, you'll also
guide them through onboarding, ensure they adopt our solutions, and
aid in their growth. As a Customer Architect, you'll stand as the
Go-to Technical Counsel, collaborating closely with the customer and
partnering with teams like Field and Services. Your role ensures that
Elastic's offerings consistently surpass customer hopes. Leveraging
your technical knowledge, business acumen, and commitment to value,
you'll enhance and elevate the customer journey.",
            "metadata": {
                "url": "https://jobs.elastic.co/jobs/csm/united-
states/customer-architect/5112021?gh_jid=5112021#/",
                "data_type": "web_page",
                "hash": "832c08a036185237195ac37a6133db16"
            },
            "embeddings": [...]
        }
    }
```

The preceding code shows a document representing a chunk extracted by Embedchain and an embeddings array using OpenAI. So ultimately, with our documentation use case, we want the data source the way it is structured in Elastic. If the user inputs `Tell me what the requirements of the Customer Architect job at Elastic are`, the question is passed from ChatGPT to Embedchain via the plugin. The plugin first queries Elasticsearch to get the most appropriate URL out of what has been crawled, and then the URL will be added dynamically by Embedchain to the context to get a generated response using GPT.

Having laid the groundwork with Elasticsearch and embedding techniques, we now shift our focus to the heart of the conversation: ChatGPT. How do we ensure that our powerful search engine seamlessly communicates with this conversationalist? Let's delve into the integration process.

Integrating with ChatGPT—creating a real-time conversationalist

In this section, we'll explore the mechanics of fusing ChatGPT with our enriched Elasticsearch dataset. By bridging these technologies, we aim to create a bot that's not just reactive but also profoundly informed by the dynamic context we've built. We'll walk through the steps of integration, ensuring that ChatGPT can fluidly access and interpret the wealth of information stored within Elasticsearch.

Handling the real-time data flow between Elasticsearch and ChatGPT

Let's start by stepping back and reminding ourselves of our desired components and flow:

1. The user only interacts with ChatGPT.
2. The user has the plugins activated.
3. The user prompt is passed to the plugin when they ask a question regarding recent information in the Elastic documentation.
4. The prompt is analyzed by the plugin, which then queries the indexes containing the crawled documentation.
5. Elasticsearch returns one or more URLs.
6. These URLs are added to the context by Embedchain.
7. Embedchain generates a response.
8. The plugin prints the response return by Embedchain in ChatGPT to the user.

So far, we have the index with the documentation—now, we have to build the ChatGPT plugin. Refer to OpenAI for the documentation as to the basics of the plugin framework (`https://platform.openai.com/docs/plugins/introduction`). We'll move forward with the assumption that you have read the documentation and understand the fundamentals required to create a plugin.

Plugin code

The plugin must comply with the OpenAI documentation to be validated and installed in ChatGPT. We will start by looking at the repository structure, and then go on to the creation of some necessary files as well as the implementation code to achieve our goal.

Repository structure

The repository structure is simple, as shown in the following screenshot:

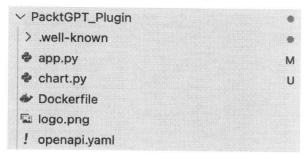

Figure 10.13: ChatGPT plugin repository structure

Let's break down the structure:

- The main service code is in `app.py`
- The plugin's logo (`logo.png`) is what will be displayed in the ChatGPT plugin store
- The plugin manifest is stored in the `ai-plugin.json` file under the `.well-known` directory
- The OpenAPI descriptor is contained in the `openapi.yaml` file

Note that we use a *Dockerfile* here as an asset to deploy the plugin. The plugin deployment platform can vary based on what you have available; I am using Google Cloud Compute. You will need to pick your preferred deployment platform or cloud provider. The plugin code deployment is beyond the scope of this book. Now, let's take a look at the code that exposes our API.

Service code

The service code is composed of four REST API endpoints expected by ChatGPT in order to validate the plugin and run the code:

```
...
@app.get("/search")
...

@app.get("/logo.png")
```

```
async def plugin_logo():
filename = 'logo.png'
return await quart.send_file(filename, mimetype='image/png')

@app.get("/.well-known/ai-plugin.json")
async def plugin_manifest():
host = request.headers['Host']
with open("./.well-known/ai-plugin.json") as f:
text = f.read()
text = text.replace("PLUGIN_HOSTNAME", f"https://{host}")
return quart.Response(text, mimetype="text/json")

@app.get("/openapi.yaml")
async def openapi_spec():
host = request.headers['Host']
with open("openapi.yaml") as f:
text = f.read()
text = text.replace("PLUGIN_HOSTNAME", f"https://{host}")
return quart.Response(text, mimetype="text/yaml")
...
```

The first /search API is the core of the implementation. The rest, in order of appearance, returns the logo, the manifest, and the OpenAPI definition.

The /search API is where the magic happens. Here is a breakdown of the implementation:

```
async def search():
  query = request.args.get("query")
  url = ESSearch(query)
  return quart.Response(url)
```

The ESSearch function is the most important part as it searches in Elasticsearch for the most relevant documents and passes their links to Embedchain to build the context. Note that we are using a simple BM25 Elasticsearch query here, as we use Embedchain to abstract the process of building the context for us. This means that Embedchain generates the embedding out of the link we are providing and returns the generated answer:

```
def ESSearch(query_text):
  cloud_url = os.environ['cloud_url']
  cid = os.environ['cloud_id']
  cp = os.environ['cloud_pass']
  cu = os.environ['cloud_user']
  es = es_connect(cid, cu, cp)
# Elasticsearch query (BM25)
  query = {
```

```
    "bool": {
      "filter": [
        {
          "prefix": {
            "url": "https://www.elastic.co/guide"
          }
        }

      ],
      "must": [{
        "match": {
          "title": {
            "query": query_text,
            "boost": 1
          }
        }
      }]
    }
}

fields = ["title", "body_content", "url"]
index = 'search-elastic-doc'
resp = es.search(index=index,
                 query=query,
                 fields=fields,
                 size=10,
                 source=False)

body = resp['hits']['hits'][0]['fields']['body_content'][0]
url = resp['hits']['hits'][0]['fields']['url'][0]
elastic_bot = App()
# Assuming 'resp' is the response object you've mentioned
for hit in resp['hits']['hits']:
  for url in hit['fields']['url']:
      print(url)
      #es_app.add(url)
      elastic_bot.add(url)

return elastic_bot.query("What can you tell me about " + query_text)
```

Note that we are keeping the prompt broad by prefixing the user input with "what can you tell me about."

Testing the code should expose an endpoint on the URL `http://0.0.0.0:5001`. Open the tool of your choice for testing and pass it a query similar to the following:

```
http://0.0.0.0:5001/search?query=detections
```

This query asks the bot to build a context about Elastic Security detections. If you print the URL in the console, you will see that Embedchain is adding content to the context:

```
https://www.elastic.co/guide/en/siem/guide/current/detection-engine-
overview.html
Successfully saved https://www.elastic.co/guide/en/siem/guide/current/
detection-engine-overview.html (DataType.WEB_PAGE). New chunks count:
15
https://www.elastic.co/guide/en/siem/guide/current/rule-api-overview.
html
Successfully saved https://www.elastic.co/guide/en/siem/guide/current/
rule-api-overview.html (DataType.WEB_PAGE). New chunks count: 5
https://www.elastic.co/guide/en/security/current/detection-engine-
overview.html
Successfully saved https://www.elastic.co/guide/en/security/current/
detection-engine-overview.html (DataType.WEB_PAGE). New chunks count:
17
https://www.elastic.co/guide/en/security/8.9/detection-engine-
overview.html
Successfully saved https://www.elastic.co/guide/en/security/8.9/
detection-engine-overview.html (DataType.WEB_PAGE). New chunks count:
17
https://www.elastic.co/guide/en/security/current/rule-api-overview.
html
Successfully saved https://www.elastic.co/guide/en/security/current/
rule-api-overview.html (DataType.WEB_PAGE). New chunks count: 5
https://www.elastic.co/guide/en/security/current/detections-
permissions-section.html
Successfully saved https://www.elastic.co/guide/en/security/current/
detections-permissions-section.html (DataType.WEB_PAGE). New chunks
count: 18
```

Again, for the purposes of this example, we keep the Elasticsearch query pretty broad in order to avoid narrowing down the results too much, but the SoC is definitely affected here, as the accuracy might decrease. So, depending on what you are looking for, you may need to fine-tune the query to produce fewer or more results.

The REST call should return something about Elastic detections:

```
Detections are alerts that are created based on rules in the Elastic
Security Solution. These alerts are generated automatically when
events and external alerts are sent to Elastic Security. They are
displayed on the Detections page, and provide information about
potential security threats or suspicious activities. For more detailed
information about the differences between events, external alerts, and
detection alerts, you can refer to the Elastic Glossary.
```

At this stage, we have validated that the endpoint is functional. We now need to describe our plugin for OpenAI.

Manifest

The manifest describes what your plugin is going to achieve and gives a direction to the model that tells when to trigger the plugin depending on the prompt that is submitted by the user. Here is the JSON content:

```json
{
"schema_version": "v1",
"name_for_human": "PacktGPT_Plugin",
"name_for_model": "PacktGPT_Plugin",
"description_for_human": "An Assistant, you know, for searching in the
Elastic documentation",
"description_for_model": "Get most recent elastic documentation post
2021 release, anything after release 7.15",
"auth": {
"type": "none"
},
"api": {
"type": "openapi",
"url": "PLUGIN_HOSTNAME/openapi.yaml",
"is_user_authenticated": false
},
"logo_url": "PLUGIN_HOSTNAME/logo.png",
"contact_email": "info@info.co",
"legal_info_url": "http://www.example.com/legal"
}
```

All the preceding fields help describe in detail the plugin we are publishing in ChatGPT, such as the name of the plugin or the URL to get the description of the API, or even the email to contact the developer. The most notable one is `description_for_model`, as this is the one the ChatGPT framework uses to guide the model in terms of what is expected from it.

The plugin description helps ChatGPT to understand what the plugin is providing and to set the behavior of the model. We now have to describe what the exposed APIs are in the plugin.

OpenAPI definition

The OpenAPI definition is a standard representation of the API exposed by the plugin, including the paths, HTTP verb, and relative parameters, as you can see in the following snippet:

```
openapi: 3.0.1
info:
title: PacktGPT_Plugin
```

```
description: Retrieve information from the most recent Elastic
documentation
version: 'v1'
servers:
- url: PLUGIN_HOSTNAME
paths:
/search:
get:
operationId: search
summary: retrieves the document matching the query
parameters:
- in: query
name: query
schema:
type: string
description: use to filter relevant part of the elasticsearch
documentations
responses:
"200":
description: OK
```

Having established a seamless integration between ChatGPT and Elasticsearch, our next step is to look at how this solution is rolled out in real-world scenarios. As we transition to the topics of deployment and extensions, we'll discuss strategies for deploying our dynamic conversationalist and also brainstorm ways to further enhance its capabilities.

Deployment

As we near the completion of publishing our plugin in ChatGPT, our next move involves setting our solution live. This section dives into deploying our plugin in ChatGPT. This is a very simple process on the ChatGPT side, but you have to deploy your code on a public endpoint so that ChatGPT can call the different endpoints exposed by your code not only to run the code but also to verify whether the plugin is compliant.

You can follow this guide I have written on how to deploy the plugin on GCP: `https://www.elastic.co/blog/chatgpt-elasticsearch-plugin-elastic-data`.

There are plenty of other options, including using Replit (`https://replit.com/`)—a browser-based IDE that can run the code and expose public API—or deploying the code in a cloud provider of your choice (Azure, GCP, AWS). I leave it to you to choose what you are comfortable with.

For what concerns ChatGPT, just go to `https://chat.openai.com/`, click on the **Plugin** dropdown, and scroll down to **Plugin store**:

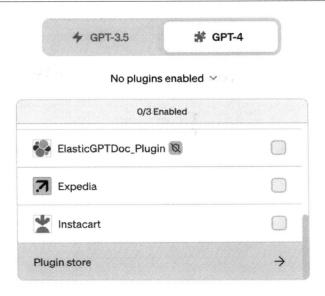

Figure 10.14: ChatGPT Plugin dropdown

Click on **Plugin store**, as shown in the previous screenshot, and in the window that appears, locate and click on **Develop your own plugin** in the bottom-right of the screen:

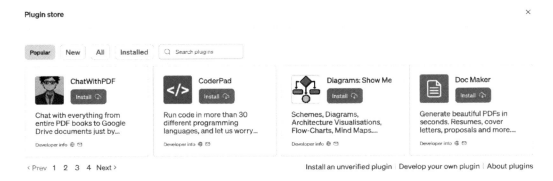

Figure 10.15: ChatGPT Plugin store

In the window that appears, copy the URL exposed by your plugin, paste it into the text field, and click on **Find manifest file**:

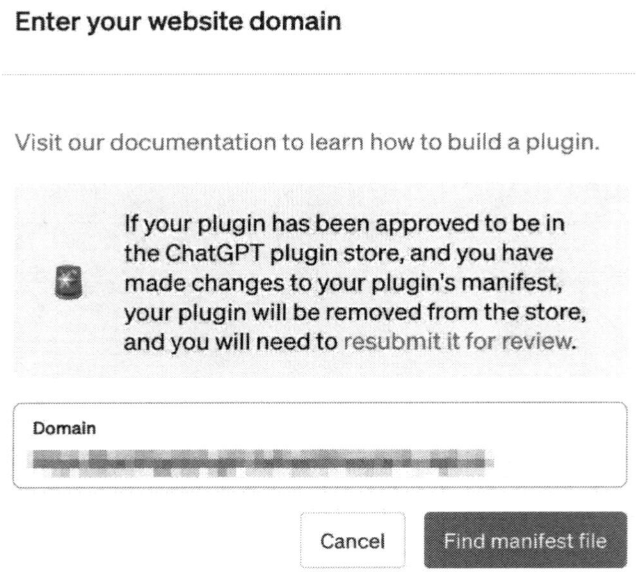

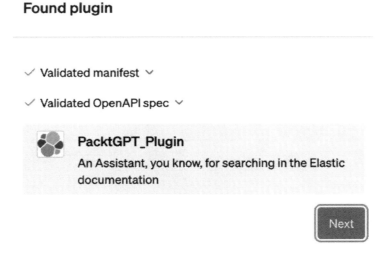

Enter your website domain

Visit our documentation to learn how to build a plugin.

> If your plugin has been approved to be in the ChatGPT plugin store, and you have made changes to your plugin's manifest, your plugin will be removed from the store, and you will need to resubmit it for review.

Domain

Cancel   Find manifest file

Figure 10.16: ChatGPT Plugin manifest finder

Your plugin should be validated, as shown in the following screenshot. Click **Next** to continue the installation steps:

Found plugin

✓ Validated manifest ⌄

✓ Validated OpenAPI spec ⌄

PacktGPT_Plugin
An Assistant, you know, for searching in the Elastic documentation

Next

Figure 10.17: ChatGPT Plugin retrieval confirmation

Go through the plugin installation until the plugin is installed and appears in the list. Make sure the plugin is checked to enable it:

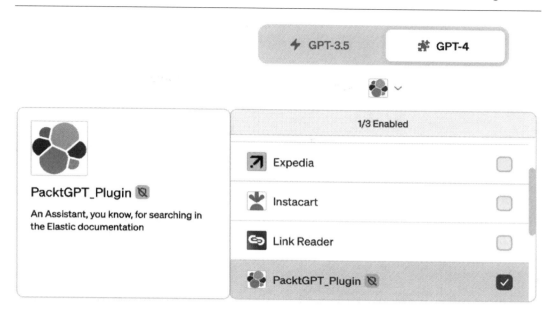

Figure 10.18: ChatGPT plugin installed and available in the list

You can now enjoy the power of a dynamic layer in ChatGPT through your new plugin, allowing you to simply prompt ChatGPT for the most recent Elastic documentation of your choice. It should trigger your plugin and give you an answer in return. An example is shown in the following screenshot:

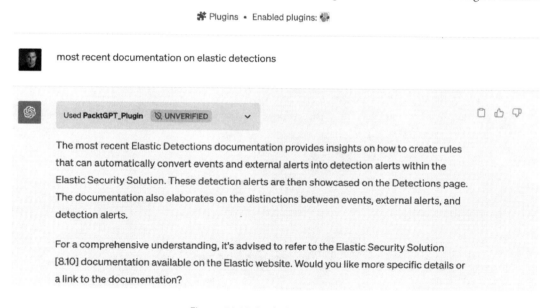

Figure 10.19: PacktGPT plugin test

You now have control over the context ChatGPT is learning from thanks to the combination of Elastic and Embedchain!

Summary

As we close this chapter on integrating dynamic context into ChatGPT, it's fitting to reflect on the broader themes we've tackled throughout this book. We embarked on a journey that weaved through the intricacies of large language models, the immense potential of Elasticsearch, and the power of contextual information to enhance user experiences.

Our venture into creating a ChatGPT plugin to dynamically pull the latest Elastic documentation represents the pinnacle of the union between static knowledge and live data. The ability to access, understand, and respond using the most recent information changes the essence of the dynamics of user-chatbot interactions, making them more timely, relevant, and impactful.

But this final chapter is merely one application in a vast landscape of possibilities. With tools such as Embedchain, the doors have been opened wide for developers and enthusiasts alike to innovate, experiment, and push the boundaries of what conversational AI can achieve when integrated with real-time data sources.

While we've covered vast ground, remember that technology is ever-evolving. The landscape we see today will be transformed tomorrow. The tools, techniques, and best practices will continue to evolve. Yet, integrating a depth of knowledge with the agility of real-time adaptability will always be at the heart of next-generation conversational AI.

I highly recommend you continue your journey of vector search with Elastic by browsing the Elastic Search Labs, the new dedicated mini-site by Elastic, here: `https://www.elastic.co/search-labs`

As this book draws to a close, the onus now falls on you, the reader, to take these learnings, insights, and tools to craft the next breakthrough in AI conversations. As you move forward, remember to keep pushing boundaries, stay curious, and, most importantly, never stop learning.

Index

www.packtpub.com

Subscribe to our online digital library for full access to over 7,000 books and videos, as well as industry leading tools to help you plan your personal development and advance your career. For more information, please visit our website.

Why subscribe?

- Spend less time learning and more time coding with practical eBooks and Videos from over 4,000 industry professionals

- Improve your learning with Skill Plans built especially for you

- Get a free eBook or video every month

- Fully searchable for easy access to vital information

- Copy and paste, print, and bookmark content

Did you know that Packt offers eBook versions of every book published, with PDF and ePub files available? You can upgrade to the eBook version at packtpub.com and as a print book customer, you are entitled to a discount on the eBook copy. Get in touch with us at customercare@packtpub.com for more details.

At www.packtpub.com, you can also read a collection of free technical articles, sign up for a range of free newsletters, and receive exclusive discounts and offers on Packt books and eBooks.

Other Books You May Enjoy

If you enjoyed this book, you may be interested in these other books by Packt:

Machine Learning with PyTorch and Scikit-Learn

Sebastian Raschka, Yuxi (Hayden) Liu, Vahid Mirjalili

ISBN: 978-1-80181-931-2

- Explore frameworks, models, and techniques for machines to 'learn' from data
- Use scikit-learn for machine learning and PyTorch for deep learning
- Train machine learning classifiers on images, text, and more
- Build and train neural networks, transformers, and boosting algorithms
- Discover best practices for evaluating and tuning models
- Predict continuous target outcomes using regression analysis
- Dig deeper into textual and social media data using sentiment analysis

Graph Machine Learning

Claudio Stamile, Aldo Marzullo, Enrico Deusebio

ISBN: 978-1-80020-449-2

- Write Python scripts to extract features from graphs
- Distinguish between the main graph representation learning techniques
- Learn how to extract data from social networks, financial transaction systems, for text analysis, and more
- Implement the main unsupervised and supervised graph embedding techniques
- Get to grips with shallow embedding methods, graph neural networks, graph regularization methods, and more
- Deploy and scale out your application seamlessly

Packt is searching for authors like you

If you're interested in becoming an author for Packt, please visit `authors.packtpub.com` and apply today. We have worked with thousands of developers and tech professionals, just like you, to help them share their insight with the global tech community. You can make a general application, apply for a specific hot topic that we are recruiting an author for, or submit your own idea

Share Your Thoughts

Now you've finished *Vector Search for Practitioners with Elastic*, we'd love to hear your thoughts! Scan the QR code below to go straight to the Amazon review page for this book and share your feedback or leave a review on the site that you purchased it from.

`https://packt.link/r/1805121022`

Your review is important to us and the tech community and will help us make sure we're delivering excellent quality content.

Download a free PDF copy of this book

Thanks for purchasing this book!

Do you like to read on the go but are unable to carry your print books everywhere?

Is your eBook purchase not compatible with the device of your choice?

Don't worry, now with every Packt book you get a DRM-free PDF version of that book at no cost.

Read anywhere, any place, on any device. Search, copy, and paste code from your favorite technical books directly into your application.

The perks don't stop there, you can get exclusive access to discounts, newsletters, and great free content in your inbox daily

Follow these simple steps to get the benefits:

1. Scan the QR code or visit the link below

https://packt.link/free-ebook/9781805121022

2. Submit your proof of purchase
3. That's it! We'll send your free PDF and other benefits to your email directly

Made in United States
Orlando, FL
13 December 2023

40776524R00133